# *The Handbook of* AMHERST

# *The Handbook of* AMHERST

*New Edition of the Classic*


Frederick H. Hitchcock

*Edited by Richard Panchyk*



THE History PRESS

Published by The History Press
Charleston, SC 29403
www.historypress.net



*Front cover:* Amherst College. *Courtesy of the editor's collection.*
*Back cover:* Amherst, 1886. *Courtesy of the Library of Congress.*

First published 1891
The History Press edition 2007

Manufactured in the United States

ISBN 978.1.59629.295.6

Library of Congress Cataloging-in-Publication Data

Hitchcock, Frederick H. (Frederick Hills), 1867-1928.
The handbook of Amherst / Frederick H. Hitchcock ; edited by Richard Panchyk. -- New ed.
p. cm.
Originally published by the author in 1891. New foreword and eleven new images.
Includes bibliographical references.
ISBN-13: 978-1-59629-295-6 (alk. paper)
1. Amherst (Mass.)--Description and travel. 2. Amherst (Mass.)--History. 3. Amherst (Mass.)--Pictorial works. 4. Connecticut River Valley--History, Local. I. Title.
F74.A5H59 2007
917.44'23--dc22
2007036771

# Contents

# Editor's Introduction

What makes this book worthy of reprinting, I think, is its compact size. A great many town histories and guides of the nineteenth century were quite voluminous and filled with extensive details. This book provides a nice summary of Amherst town and college history, along with a summary of highlights of nearby natural wonders and concise descriptions of the surrounding towns. It is an interesting little window into Amherst life in the late nineteenth century.

In 1891, Amherst was a college town, just as it is today, only on a much smaller scale. There were only hundreds of students instead of the more than twenty-five thousand of today. Amherst and the immediate vicinity are now nationally famous for their "Five Colleges" and local residents are long accustomed to the presence of students and the vibrance they bring to Amherst from September through May. The college life extends to neighboring towns in all directions—from South Hadley to Sunderland. Local businesses thrive and tourism is strong. The reader of this book will note both similarities and differences in the Amherst of the past and of the present when reading this little guide.

I have provided notes on various points throughout the book. These are not intended to be comprehensive updates and explanations of everything that happened since 1891. I certainly did not intend to chart the fate of each of the buildings mentioned in Hitchcock's book; suffice it to say that some have been demolished, but a good many are still standing. I have chosen to elaborate upon or update selected names, events and places mentioned in the book, hopefully to the benefit and not the burden of the reader.

The reader should also note that the spelling and grammar of the original edition has not been changed or corrected. Some of the smaller, lesser quality illustrations have not been reproduced here, and a few additional illustrations (such as the one on the cover) have been added. These are marked in the caption as *Image courtesy of editor's collection* or *Image courtesy of Library of Congress.* All other illustrations are from the original edition and thus date to 1891. The placement of illustrations within the original edition has been enhanced to move the images closer to the relevant text.

I hope that, as Amherst approaches its 250th anniversary, this guide can serve as both a reminder of Amherst's glorious past and a beacon of good things to come in the future.

Richard Panchyk
September 2007

# Author's Introduction

*The Handbook of Amherst* has been prepared in the hope of affording its readers a comprehensive view of one of the most attractive little towns of Western Massachusetts; and it is believed to be the first attempt at combining in one volume the matters of permanent interest to residents, strangers, and college students alike.

While the information, covering this broad field, is greatly condensed in order to produce a book of convenient size, no effort has been spared to make it accurate, as well as complete in every detail.

Other than that of being a "handbook," the volume has no pretensions. With it as a guide, the visitor to Amherst can see everything of any importance in the town and the surrounding country; and to both residents and students it should prove a valuable companion.

Without the assistance of many of the friends of the town and its colleges, the publication of the book in its present form would not have been possible. The names of all those who have aided in gathering material, and in correcting the manuscript and proofs, cannot be mentioned, but among them were: Dr. William S. Tyler, President M.E. Gates, President H.H. Goodell, Dr. Edward Hitchcock, William A. Dickinson, Esq.,[1] Professor Charles Wellington, Professor W.P. Brooks, Charles O. Parmenter, and Rev. D. W. Marsh. To these and many others, whose suggestions have been most valuable, cordial acknowledgments of their kindness are due.

The photographs, from which the large majority of the illustrations were made, were the work of Mr. J.L. Lovell, of Amherst. A few were furnished by H.N. Potter, of the class of 1891 in Amherst College, and by the Notman Photographic Company of Boston. A number of the illustrations of scenes outside of Amherst, that otherwise would not have been presented here, are loaned by Wade, Warner & Co., of Northhampton, from "Picturesque Hampshire." A picture from the "92 Olio" is also used.

Amherst, Massachusetts,
June, eighteen hundred and ninety-one

A panoramic view of Amherst as it appeared in 1886, just a few years before this book was first published. *Image courtesy of Library of Congress.*

# , MASS.

23 Amity Street School.
24 First National Bank.
25 Amherst Savings Bank & Post Office.
26 Palmer's Hall.
27 Masonic & G. A. R. Halls.
28 New London Northern R. R. Station.
29 Amherst House, Edward Conkey, Prop.
30 Ward's Hotel, Frank P. Wood, Prop.
31 Sisson's Hotel, T. T. Sisson, Prop.
32 H. D. Fearing & Co., Straw Goods Man'f'g.
33 The Hills Company, Straw Goods Man'f'g.
34 L. B. Dickinson, Planing Mill & Box Factory.
35 Amherst Gas Company.

College Societies.

36 Beta Theta Pi.
37 Chi Psi.
38 Delta Kappa Epsilon.
39 Delta Upsilon.
40 Psi Upsilon.
41 Chi Phi.
42 Alpha Delta Phi.
43 Theta Delta Chi.

# AMHERST OF THE PAST.

Chapter 1

# Amherst of the Past

Amherst was settled from the west. It lies among the lower foot-hills of the Green Mountains, east of old Hadley, of which it long formed a part. It took one hundred years for the tide of English immigration to get less than one hundred miles inland from the shores of Massachusetts to Amherst. The movement, like that of the Pilgrims through Holland to Plymouth Rock, was roundabout, first southeastward, into the State of Connecticut; thence northward, along the river to Hadley; and finally eastward, involving the entrance to Amherst from the west.

The original settlers, coming mainly from Hadley and from Hatfield, then a part of Hadley, were nearly all the descendants of the earliest Hadley settlers. Their ancestors, with a few exceptions, had come from England to Massachusetts Bay between 1631 and 1635, and finding near the shore less land and less freedom than they wished, sent explorers, in 1633, by land and water to the Connecticut River. In 1635 and 1636 they moved through the wilderness to the fertile valley, settling at Wethersfield and Hartford. There they remained for almost a generation, until religious disputes in 1759 and 1760 led a part of the body to move to Hadley.

It is interesting to look back upon the principles which caused the division of the Connecticut settlements. The differences at Hartford occasioning the up-river movement sprang largely from divergent theories of government. The friends of Rev. John Hooker, known in England as the light of the western churches,[2] sought to obtain a larger personal liberty denied them at Hartford. The first lecture of this good man at Hartford sounded a note that should never be forgotten in the history of liberty in Massachusetts and Connecticut, and it foreshadowed in a wonderful manner the truths which lay at the basis of the Federal government founded more than a century later.

On a Thursday, the 1st of May, 1638, his text was, "Take you wise men, and understanding, and known among your tribes, and I will make them rulers over you" (Deut. i. 13). He laid down "Doctrine 1. That the choice of the public magistrates belongs unto the people by God's own allowance. 2. The privilege of election which belongs to the people, therefore, must be exercised not according to their humors, but according to the blessed will and law of God. 3. They who have power to appoint officers and magistrates, it is their power also to set bounds and limitations of the power and place to which they call them." And he gave as reasons: "1. Because the foundation of authority is laid firstly in the free consent of the people. 2. Because, by a free choice, the hearts of the people will be more inclined to the laws of the persons, and more ready to yield."

On such broad principles were the early inhabitants of the Connecticut Valley nurtured, and such principles were especially cherished by the parents and grandparents of the first settlers of Amherst.

Sixty-eight years intervened between the occupation of Hadley in 1659 and the settlement of Amherst, although the lands of the latter place were more elevated, lay but four miles away, and were within the boundaries of the town.

The history of Hadley's own "Middle Street" makes this fact not at all surprising. It was not occupied for fifty-three years after the "West Street," and in 1720 it had only twenty families. The lots were first laid out by vote of the town in 1684. In 1687 most of them were given to inhabitants of the town on condition that they build within three years. An Indian war breaking out the following year, no one dared live outside of the fortifications; and the grants had to be renewed in 1690 and 1692, only to be further delayed in their settlement by the French and Indian War until 1713.[3]

In addition to the motive of personal safety, the wish to be near the common meeting-house, and to perpetuate the home and village life of England, did much to influence the people to move, when they did move, in large rather than in small bodies. The flow of population from England was checked about that time, thus retarding the growth of the colonies away from the seacoast.

It is very clear that the Hadley settlers did not realize the value of the land lying at a distance from the river. They complained in 1673 that most of their woodland was a "barren pine-plain, capable of very little improvement," and accordingly their boundaries were widened by the General Court so as to "run five miles up the river and five miles down the river and six miles from their meeting-house eastward." This grant gave them all the land now included in the town of Amherst, but ten years after they begged for more, saying that "the inhabitants are shut up on the east and north by a desolate and barren desert," and "the young people are straightened for want of enlargement and remove to remote places" rather than live in Amherst. This petition brought them in May, 1683, an addition four miles square between Hadley and Springfield, extending eastward from the Connecticut River. It proved useless to them during the Indian wars, and was not even surveyed until 1715.

The following vote, passed by the town of Hadley on the 4th of March, 1700, may still be deciphered in the old record-book, and it shaped for all the time the positions of the main streets and the lots of Amherst, then known as East Hadley:

> *Voted by the town, that three miles and one-quarter eastward from the meeting-house, and so from the north side of Mount Holyoke unto Mill River, shall lye as common lands forever, supposing that the line will take in the new swamp.*
>
> *Voted, that the rest of the commons, eastward, shall be laid out in three divisions, that is to say, between the road leading to Brookfield, and the Mill River, notwithstanding there is liberty for the cutting of wood and timber so long as it lieth unfenced; there is likewise to*

> *be left between every division forty rods[4] for highways, and what will be necessary to be left for highways eastward and West through every division, is to be left to the discretion of the measurers; and every one to have a proportion in the third division, and every householder to have a 50-pound allotment and all others who are now the proper inhabitants of Hadley, 16 years old and upward, to have a 25-pound allotment in said commons.*

Rendered into language that is more intelligible at the present day, this vote meant to reserve forever as common property the tract of land lying between Mount Holyoke on the south, and Mill River on the north, and extending from the "West Street" of Hadley eastward to a north and south line three and a quarter miles from the meeting-house, then standing in the middle of the street. The land east of this "Inner Commons," the present Amherst, was to be divided into three sections separated by highways running north and south, which are now represented by Pleasant and East streets, and these to be intersected by cross-streets, running east and west.

Things moved slowly in those days, and it was three years later—May, 1703—when the town measurers announced that the instruction of the vote had been carried out. Portions of East Hadley were allotted to individuals, whether they became settlers or remained in the old street, and the same names occur in the record of this division of land as may be found in the later division of South Hadley. The allotments were not made so much for immediate settlement as to allow the separate ownership of wood, pasture, and swamp lands, and most of those who were given lots never intended to reside upon them. So it was not until 1727 or 1728 that the new territory began to be occupied, although tradition related that a hardy woodsman named Foote attempted unsuccessfully to live by fishing and trapping near what is known as "East Street." For years that portion of the town lying just north of the Second Congregational meeting-house had the name of "Foote's Folly Swamp."

The three divisions of East Hadley are plainly indicated to-day by the two north and south roads, of which the village common and the East Street are parts. Both of these highways, originally forty rods wide, have been narrowed from time to time as the roadways became improved, and there was less need of making detours to avoid the hummocks and treacherous mud-holes which first rendered travelling sinuous. Recent measurements made for the Handbook of Amherst locate this west highway as lying between the stone carriage block in from of the Amherst House on Amity Street and the residence of H.B. Edwards on Lessey Street. The present position of Amity Street is nearly that of the middle one of the three cross-highways laid out in the same width. In 1754, Hadley reduced the west street to twenty rods' width, and the east street to twelve, and a large part of the business of the precinct meetings for fifteen years—from 1767 to 1782—was to discontinue parts of these broad highways.

The first of the three divisions was bounded by the line, "three miles and one-quarter from the Meeting-house," at Hadley and the west street, now Pleasant Street; the second division lay between the west and east streets, and the third extended a mile from the east street to the Pelham hills. The first two were two hundred and forty rods wide, and all stretched from the Bay road on the south to the Mill River on the north. Ninety-seven persons received lots in either the first or the second divisions, and all were given sections in the third for pasture land.

The first authentic record that the grants of land in East Hadley had been occupied is in the vote of Hadley, January 5, 1730, to lay out an "acre of land for a cemetery for the "east inhabitants," who are known to have numbered at that time eighteen families. The names of these early settlers are John Ingram, Sr., John Ingram, Jr., Ebenezer Kellogg, John Cowls, Jonathan Cowls, Samuel Boltwood, Samuel Hawley, Nathaniel Church, John Wells, Aaron Smith, Nathaniel Smith, Richard Chauncey, Stephen Smith, John Nash, Jr., Joseph Wells, Ebenezer Scovil, Ebenezer Ingram, Ebenezer Dickinson. Twelve of these men came from Hadley, and the others from Hatfield.

The first step toward the separation of the two settlements was taken in 1733, when Hadley voted that the "east inhabitants have a part of their taxes abated upon their hiring a minister of their own," previous to this every one being obliged to make the journey to the meeting-house old Hadley for Sabbath worship. The parishes were finally divided by an act of the General Court, December 31, 1734, making East Hadley the "Third Precinct" of Hadley on the condition of its settling a "learned orthodox minister," and erecting a meeting-house. The decree of the General Court bounded the new precinct, it "Being of the contents of two miles and three-quarters in breadth, and seven miles in length, bounded Westerly on a tract of land reserved by the town of Hadley, to lye as common forever, Southerly on Boston road, Easterly on Equivalent lands, and Northerly on the town of Sunderland."

While the church affairs of the precinct thus became distinct from those of the parent village, town business was still transacted in the original settlement, and the town officers were almost entirely from that place.

The first minister of the Third Precinct, the Rev. David Parsons, who was born at Malden, began his labors in November, 1735, settling permanently four years later, when he was given money and land for building a house, and was promised 100 pounds salary, with an increase in proportion to the growth of the population. The meeting-house begun in 1738 was located upon the site of the present college Observatory, and, although not completed until 1753, was occupied some time prior to 1742. The history of this First Congregational Church is traced at some length in another portion of this book. It suffices to say here that its development and growth were parallel with the development and growth of the town, the paths diverging only when later religious differences resulted in the establishment of the Second Parish, and the town, as a political body, discontinued its support of public worship.

In 1739 Oliver Partridge resurveyed the town of Hadley, determining what still remains the eastern boundary of Amherst. He followed the provisions of the grant to Hadley in 1673, finding the point exactly six miles east of the old meeting-house, and running by compass a north and south line through it. The first surveyors had done their work without a compass, but they were in reality more accurate than Partridge, for the magnetic variation changed the line so that the lots in the southern part of the third division were widened considerably, while those at the north were narrowed. To offset this loss of territory, the town allowed about six hundred acres on the Flat Hills to those who had suffered by the relocation of the line.

The Third Precinct of Hadley sent its share of men to the Indian wars that raged intermittently up and down the beautiful valley of the Connecticut between the years of 1744 and 1763. Many brave men were sacrificed, but among those surviving, several gained the prominence and ability that placed them at the front at the opening of the Revolutionary War.

The year 1749 finds the first indication that the settlement is alive to the necessity of providing the rising generation with opportunities for gaining some education. Appropriations, liberal for the times, were made "to Hire three School Dames for three or four Months in the Summer seson to Larne children to read." The pupils met at the teachers' homes, for there were no school-houses until after 1764, when four were ordered to be built, a "North, a South, a West Middle, and a South East Middle." Josiah Pierce began to teach October 27, 1765. He was the first school-master, and spent part of the year at each of the "Middle" school-houses. A graduate of Harvard College, he was paid $5.33 a month, adding to this by keeping an evening school, and preaching at the churches of the surrounding places for twenty shillings a Sunday. It is not at all surprising that "he dismissed his school in disgust March 29, 1769," as the records have it. The school-house of this working pedagogue stood upon the village common near the spot now marked by the watering-trough. In 1784 Amherst voted "to set up six schools." It is interesting to notice that before Amherst College graduated a single student, thirty-nine Amherst boys had obtained degrees, thirteen from Williams, ten from Dartmouth, seven from Yale, and three from Harvard.[5]

Owing to the incorporation of South Hadley as a district in 1753, the name "East Hadley" was changed to the "Second Precinct of Hadley," and six years later, just a century after the founding of Hadley, the "Second Precinct" was made a district. Governor Pownall, in signing the act of incorporation, February 13, 1759, gave it the name of Amherst, in honor of General Jeffrey Amherst, prominent at that time as the commander of the memorable expedition against Louisburg, and still later commander-in-chief and field marshal of the English armies.[6] In 1776 General Amherst was created a baron.

The new district held its first legal meeting March 19, 1759. From that time on, the spirit of independence and thrift seemed to take a firmer hold upon the people. They toiled diligently for the betterment of their estates, laying aside the generous store of English money that was to prove so useful during the hard times of the approaching war.

Much of the public business previously centering exclusively in the mother settlement was transferred to Amherst, with the beneficial results always attending an interest in home affairs. In 1758 the white population actually outnumbered that of Hadley, and in 1776 had become some two hundred greater than in any of the surrounding villages. Nearly all the material conditions of the district surpassed those of the three villages which originally belonged to Hadley.

Regular communication was opened with Boston in 1767 by the enterprise of Simeon Smith, an Amherst citizen. Previous to that time all travelling had been done

Amherst was named after the French and Indian War hero Lord Jeffrey Amherst.

on horseback; but Smith possessed a wagon that is recorded as being strong enough to bear a ton of freight. He made a trip, by way of the old Bay road, in about a week, and found sufficient trade to bring him a good profit, the most remunerative part of his business being the importation of great quantities of New England rum.

Youthful Amherst was not without its "ordinaries," or taverns, even in the days of its smallest population. Ebenezer Kellogg was licensed in 1734, as the first ordinary-keeper. He kept his place for only three years, but within the next few years his successors were so numerous that a record of them would be wearisome.[7] At the time he opened his tavern, the men of the town numbered twenty-nine, and only three hundred and fifty acres of land had been cleared and improved. One groggery for every sixty persons, the records say, was the proportion in 1783, when there were seven hundred inhabitants.

All this time the residents on the outskirts of the district had been journeying several miles each Sabbath day to attend church services in the village. In 1772 they united in advocating a division of the original parish so that the north and south sections of the district should each have a church, the one in the centre to be discontinued. The same instincts that influence men to-day were no less active then, and the prospect of having their place of worship removed to an inconvenient distance so alarmed the villagers that they begged the General Court to interfere in the matter. Their petition was an able document. The records show that a committee from the august body of legislators visited Amherst in March, 1774, but their report and the entire question was soon forgotten in the excitement of the war immediately following. Church matters did not become prominent again until 1781. A part of the parish withdrew in accordance with a vote passed October 15, 1782, and constituted themselves the Second Congregational Parish. They had opposed the selection of Rev. David Parsons, Jr., to succeed his father as pastor, but were overruled by the majority. The incorporation of this new parish marked the end of the control of religious affairs by the district.

Amherst assumed the privileges of a town about this time by electing Nathaniel Dickinson, Jr., a representative to the Provincial Congress, which met successively at Salem, Concord, and Cambridge. The name of "town," used without authority in the records after 1776, was legalized by a general law of the State in 1876.

Amherst must have proved a warm place for the Tories of the Revolutionary times. The character of the American ancestry of the early settlers of Hadley and Amherst, especially of that from Hartford, would lead one to find men ready to stand up for freedom and at the risk of life and property. With most of the men of Amherst this was true, but, as in not a few cases elsewhere, the highly educated classes were more loyal to the king of England and opposed to the popular idea of freedom, than the body of the people. The names of these opponents of the war included many of the leading citizens, at the head of whom was no less a personage than the Rev. David Parsons, Sr. Besides censuring and even imprisoning several of these obnoxious persons for being "notoriously inimical to liberty," the town voted to support whatever action the Continental Congress might take for the safety of the colonies, and in January, 1776, actually deprived those "not owning independence of the crown of Great Britain" of the right of voting upon town matters.

Even if former leaders be lukewarm and hostile at the time of a revolution in thought or action, the people find new men to go before in the paths they are determined to tread. It was so at Amherst. Men less polished than collegians, some of them diamonds in the rough, profane, came to the front in place of the more accomplished list scholars and gentlemen.

These men entered into correspondence with the Committee of Correspondence at Boston. Having "Red and Considered" the letter from Boston, they voted, March 14, 1774, to send a reply. Their letter was not a triumph of spelling or oratory, but it was a mine of sturdy sense. They had no more respect for capitals than for kings. One may not forget that Noah Webster and his spelling-book had not yet neared, and often in the antique dress of the letters of the time there is something so grotesque as to cause a smile; but one feels, when reading the quaint spelling, much as did Dr. Holmes at the sight of the man, in "The Last Leaf"[8]:

*I know it is a sin*
*For me to sit and grin*
*At him here;*
*But the old three-cornered hat,*
*And the breeches,—and all that,—*
*Are so queer.*

But, after all, our own spelling is unreasonable, and the letter of the patriots is too earnest for more than momentary merriment. This is what they wrote:

> *To the Respectable Committee of Correspondence in the town of Boston.*
> *Gentn.: We think it needless to Recapitulate all those grievancses Which we suffer in Common with our opprest Brethren and Neighbors. Sufficient to Say that tho we have been Long silent we are not insensible of the oppressions we suffer and the ruin which threatens us or regardlis of the Diabolical Designs of our Mercenary and Manevolent Enemies Foreign and Domestic and are ready not onley to risque but even to Sacrifice our Lives and Properties in Defence of our just rights & liberties at Present we are only Galled not subdued and think ourselves heapy in having such vigilant and faithfull gardians of our rights in the Metropolis on hoom we Can Depend to Call on us in Season to unite with our suffering Countrymen in the Common Cause of America we hope and beg that you will Still Persevere in that most Honorrble & importent Imployment of watching over us with the Same Care and Fidelity which has hitherto Distinguish,d & grately Dignified your Characters in the Estimation of all who have a just sence of that best of Blessings Liberty & an Equal abhorence of that tame submition which tends to Entail on our Posterrity that worst of Curses Slavery.*
>
> *Every Avenue to the Royal Ear seems to be blocked up by the gross falsities & Designd Misrepresentations of those from sum of whom at Least we might have Expected better things but there is a King who Cannot be Deceived & who will not be mocked who has pointed out a never failing resource when Petitions & Remonstances, Truth & justice*

*are unsuccessfully opposed to Tironey and Oppression falsehood & Corruption & when you feel that impulse which will not brook longer Delay, the wisdum of the People will naturally write in mode of the best Appeal, to which you most Distant Brethren Expect to be summoned unless prevent,d by a sudding unexpected & very favourable Chandge of affears. their are whom justice forbids to live but whom we would spare to Convince the world we Despise their utmost hate &- malicious Cunning. the Colonies united are invinciably free & we dout not you are Convinc,d that the Preservation of that union outweighs every other Consideration and is at Present our most Important Concern. while that is secure we have nothing to fear but may Laugh at all attempts to Enslave us we know of no punishment which Can be Inflicted on those vilens in Exalted Stations adequate to their own reflections & remorse accompanyd with our Neglect, Contempt & Detestation but at the same time should think ourselves happier if Everey banefull Noxious weed Could by aney means be Eradicated from this our fair garden of Liberty. we Entirely approve & Concurr with you in every measure hitherto adopted & Conducted & return our gratefull thanks to the People of Boston & the Neighboring towns in a Perticuler manner for the seasonable Indeavours & mandley opposition to prevent the Landing of the East India Companys teas which plan we are Convinc,d was artefully Projected to open the gate for the admition of Tyrany & oppression with all their Rapacious followers to Stalk at Large &- uncontrol,d to Ravage our fare & Dear bought Possessions. Everey measure which shall appear Conducive to the Publick good we are warranted to assure you will always be approved & support,d by a Large Majorrity in this District and* [y?]*our Continual Correspondence as Long as you shall think occasion requires meet with Due respect & attention we are in behalf of the District very Respectfully Gent'm your oblig'd & most hble, servts*

*MOSES DICKINSON, REUBEN DICKINSON, JACOB McDANIEL, NATH'LL DICKINSON, JOSEPH WILLIAMS (committee)*[9]

Their actions fully sustained their words. The usual committees of "Correspondence," "Safety," and "Inspection" were chosen, and among the members were many who figured prominently in the affairs of the colonies. A representative was sent to the Provincial Congress, and in June, 1776, it was voted "That, should the Honorable Congress for the safety of the United Colonies in America; Declare them Independant of the Kingdom of Great Britain; we the inhabitants of the town of Amherst solemnly engage with our lives and fortunes to support them in the measure."

Following April 19, 1775, Captain Reuben Dickinson gathered a company of minute-men, who were under his call between two and four weeks, and at their disbanding he enlisted an eight-months company, of which the noted Daniel Shays of Shutesbury, the leader of the "Shays' Rebellion," was a non-commissioned officer. Amherst men joined other companies in varying numbers. A company under the command of Captain James Hendrick of Amherst obtained a good many. Captain Dickinson's command, and several of the others having men from the town, were at the battle of Bunker Hill.

Noah Webster, who lived in Amherst for ten years while working on his famous dictionary. *Image courtesy of Library of Congress.*

Later companies gathered by Captain Dickinson, Captain Harvey, and Captain Cook, from Amherst and the vicinity, were in General Gates' army, fought in the battles of September 19 and October 7, 1777, and saw the surrender of General Burgoyne. Half of the English army and the defeated general himself, passed through Hadley and along the Bay road, then the southern boundary line of the town, on their way to Boston. To this day one of the old families of Hadley are in possession of a sword presented by General Burgoyne to one of the citizens of the town.

During the campaigns of 1777 until 1781, Amherst furnished its due proportion of men, distributed through several companies, and in many instances brave and efficient officers. Liberal bounties, formally offered by the town to the enlisting men, rapidly drained the store of hard money that had been laid up by the thrifty farm folk. The Continental bills depreciated in value until in 1780 a dollar in silver would buy a hundred of them, and a year after two hundred. Old soldiers boasted after the hard times were over, that $50 had often been paid for a single meal.

The first of the rewards of the courage, with which each new deprivation of the war had been met, came, when the inhabitants of the town assembled on the 4th day of September, 1780, bringing in their votes for a governor of the new commonwealth, as follows: "The Hon'ble John Hancock Esq'r, Forty three; The Hon'ble James Bowdoin Esq'r eight."

In the State convention which ratified the Federal Constitution, the Amherst representative, Daniel Cooley, probably reflected the wishes of his constituents when he voted against ratification. There were several years about this time when the town failed to send its representatives to the General Court, and at least twice it was fined for this neglect.

An interesting description of the town in 1800 has been given in Dr. Tyler's able "History of Amherst College."[10] At that time the only store in the village stood at the corner of what afterward became Phoenix Row and North Pleasant Street. At the opposite end of the row was the house later occupied by Noah Webster.[11] A vigorous distillery stood within the square bounded by the Common and Spring and College streets, entirely at variance, happily be it said, with the present ideas of sobriety. The situation of the home of Levi Cowles, on North Pleasant Street, and of Mrs. Emerson, the Judge Strong estate, mark the former width of the two highways, for these buildings are among the few then standing.

In 1814 eight hundred acres of Hadley were added at the northwest corner of the town, and in 1815 the southern boundary was changed from the Bay road to the top of the Holyoke range. At this time there were not more than twenty-five houses in the village.[12] Until several years after the college was founded the centre of trade and enterprise was at East Amherst, and there the town-meetings were held.

Amherst became prominent in 1787 through Shays' Rebellion, which took place almost within her own borders. The deluded soldiery, under Daniel Shays, encamped and drilled upon Pelham hills, and returning from their rash attempts to defy the federal authority at Springfield and Northampton, were followed by the regular troops across the southern part of the town to the Pelham hills again, whence they dispersed northward.

To the War of 1812 the inhabitants of Amherst were bitterly opposed. Three citizens were sent to a convention of delegates from the towns of Hampshire County, and the memorial then adopted strongly solicited the federal government to come to some terms of peace with Great Britain. Notwithstanding this, the demand for troops that came later was promptly met by Amherst, as well as the other towns of the Connecticut Valley.

The war of the Rebellion sacrificed the lives of fifty-eight of the three hundred and seventy-four volunteers from Amherst; and the expenses, public and private, amounted to more than $46,000.

Chapter 2

# The Connecticut Valley

*By Mabel Loomis Todd*[13]

The mellow light of a warm August afternoon lay shimmering over a grassy meadow road. No fences divided the rich farm lands on either side from the road, or from one another. The hum and buzz of innumerable insects filled the fragrant air, while distant sounds of mowing could be heard at intervals, as the rowan was being here and there gathered in by thrifty farmers.

Nearer at hand fields of tropical-leaved tobacco sent out a slightly pungent odor, while an occasional tall stalk, crowned with its delicate pink blossoms, was allowed to ripen and go to seed in the summer sunshine.

In the eyes of two travellers, driving leisurely along this lovely way, the whole scene was richly, sensuously delightful. As they passed the fields of tobacco and of corn, a dull but continuous murmur became apparent, growing louder, until a large barn came into view, from which the sound emerged. Here a curious, and in this day somewhat unusual, sight appeared. Heavy machinery was cutting into small pieces and packing into great compressed masses the succulent cornstalks,—future food for cattle when this verdant meadow should be filled with snow and ice. In other words, ensilage was in process of manufacture. Farther on, fields of broom-corn, with airily waving tassels, bordered the highway. And everywhere were farmhouses with generous barns, large orchards in which early apples began to show sun-warmed cheeks, and old elms full of dignity and grace. Toward the west flowed a noble river, not less than eight hundred feet wide, reflecting the sky on its placid surface. Still further west, ranges of misty blue hills filled the distance, while nearer rose Mount Warner, the pioneer of all that ancient mountain brotherhood.

In the south lay the rugged and picturesque Holyoke range, and the steep sides of Mount Tom beyond the opening where the river has its passage. Northward, Mount Toby showed itself in a luminous, purple atmosphere, a rich tone modified in Sugarloaf, across the river, by its more scarred sides of red sandstone. The gentle slope Pelham and Shutesbury hills eastward was densely green, and little colored by distance.

Over all this homelike scene the caressing August sky and sunshine brooded tenderly. Where, indeed, could they find a fairer tarrying-place?

This lovely Connecticut Valley—originally the Quon-eh-ti-cut, prominent in four States, no less than twenty miles wide in Massachusetts, the garden-spot of New England, rich, fertile, and beautiful—is full of interest to the geologist, the naturalist, and the historian, as well as to him who merely appreciates the rare beauty of its scenery, or the promise of its luxuriant crops.

Pre-eminently a farming region, the valley has also many manufacturing interests, as Holyoke, Springfield, and its other cities amply testify. But its pastoral character remains, and the beauty of its sweet meadows is as yet untouched.

Many types of old New England houses abound. Hadley, Deerfield, and some of the earlier villages still preserve the colonial shapes and ornaments, the fan-lights above the doors, and the old hip and gambrel roofs. Somewhat later, a far less beautiful style came into vogue. The hall, instead of running straight-forwardly through the centre of the house, giving ample room for stairways, became contracted to a mere entrance lobby, barely large enough to contain a door into the rooms on either side, while a steep and narrow stairway was forced to contort itself cruelly in order to rise at all. These houses, however, have large, though low-ceiled rooms, and frequently, parlor cupboards in the wainscoted wall, large fireplaces, and elaborately carved window and door ornaments. Still later, came the first "modern" white, green-blinded country house with a side wing. A single path generally leads to the rarely used front door, diverging just before reaching its chilling hospitality into a branch walk to the more homelike side door, where all is cheerful and merry, where family life surges in and out over the stone doorstep, and hens peck contentedly about the short grass. Yet another style of farmhouse appears, whose long row of sheds and out-buildings reaches to an astonishing distance, terminating in an immense barn by which the modest and insignificant dwelling is completely overshadowed.

Sturdy and pious as the earlier inhabitants were, steadfast of purpose, and of noble lives, their aesthetic sense must have been very much in abeyance. Too sadly common is the fashion in this fair region, where Nature spreads her most tempting glories, of setting an uncompromising barn directly between the house and a wonderful view of mountain and vale which any summer tourist would go miles to see for an hour.[14]

The inoffensive little house is perhaps perched close to the highway, and directly across the road, in its face and eyes, rises the dignified shelter of cattle and hay, shutting off all possible outlook.

The age of the mansard roof infliction is still apparent; but later taste has displaced its ugliness, and smooth, well-kept lawns now often lead to charming houses of our own day, which, while preserving the best features of early colonial architecture, have added without and within the beauty of a more cultured and many-sided life.[15]

Very rich in flowers, ferns, and mosses is this favored valley. In late spring the shady roads are lighted by the pale pink of the laurel, set in its dark green leaves; and earlier, arbutus, hepaticas, anemones, and all the brave company of early blossoms fill the woods. Columbine and cowslips, wild azalia, scarlet "painted-cup" and pimpernel, loose strife, meadow-lilies, yellow and scarlet, give place to hosts of wild roses and clematis, while yet later come cardinal

North Hadley.

flowers and closed gentians, the tiny five-leaved gentian and its royal fringed brother, brilliant blackalder berries glowing in the sun; and last of all the weird witch-hazel holds sway in the bare November woods, companioned by airy ghosts from the milkweed pots, and spectral maiden-hair, white in its secluded recesses.

And when

*The murmuring of bees has ceased, but murmuring of some*
*Posterior, prophetic,*
*Has simultaneous come,*[16]

then,

*Besides the autumn poets sing,*
*A few prosaic days*
*A little this side of the snow,*
*And that side of the haze.*

*Still is the bustle in the brook,*
*Sealed are the spicy valves,*
*Mesmeric fingers softly touch*
*The eyes of many elves.*[17]
*–Emily Dickinson.*[18]

A merely technical list of all the floral beauties of the region would fill a goodly volume. Professor Tuckerman's catalogue of the lichens shows their rare variety and number, and the ferns are no less noteworthy.[19]

Partridges drum undisturbed in their leafy homes, the rarer quail is still a resident, and the meadows and mountain-sides echo to the songs of numberless wild birds.

Song-sparrows and bluebirds greet with throbbing music the early spring, after the longest and coldest winter has failed to drive the energetic bluejay from his covert in pine or hemlock, whence comes his "brigadier" note, with all its harshness full of cheer and hopefulness. The rose-breasted grosbeak, the pewees, the flaming orioles, the bobolink and meadow-lark, the humming-bird and linnet, the cat-bird with its lovely song, the various swallows with their startlingly swift flight, the sweet-voiced vireos and warblers,—all, and a numerous brotherhood beside, fill the crevices of every fragrant spring and summer day with their flashing wings and tender songs, voicing the winds and the woods and the waters in sweetest melody. The rare red-necked grebe, the snowy heron, and the night heron have been seen in the region, as well as the yellow-rail, the blue golden-winged warbler, and the yellowbreasted chat.

About one hundred and thirty years ago a few elms were set out here and there. Some of these pioneers still survive; but in general, attention to ornamental trees has been given within the present century. The old-time Lombardy poplar, with its stiffly sentinel aspect, and its shimmering, silvery leaves, was introduced at one time, but its representatives were generally cut down after a few years, and few now remain to give their stately dignity to any old homestead. The distinctive trees of this grassy, sunny Connecticut Valley are undoubtedly its elms. Their graceful branches appear in nearly all of the paintings of the region, and wave across the pages of the valley literature. And it has been prominent in literature since the early days, from Jonathan Edwards in his Northampton home; to the gentler if less profound philosophy of Bryant, whose "Story of the Fountain" might well have been told of the far-away spring of our noble river.[20]

Bryant's home in Cummington was one of his two favorite spots for writing his poems. His journalistic labors in New York were ever kept distinct from his deeply loved country life, where alone he would express himself in verse. The names of George Bancroft, Henry Ward Beecher,[21] and George William Curtis belong to the valley; and Dr. J.G. Holland, born in Belchertown, wrote of the region in "Kathrina," and "The Bay Path." Charles Dudley Warner[22] remembers it in some of his daintiest sketches; and here, too, linger memories of Jenny Lind,[23] whose compelling voice comes floating down the years in the traditions of a previous generation. More lately, George W. Cable's[24] increasing fame adorns the Connecticut; while to Amherst belongs the world-wide reputation of "H.H.,[25] and the posthumous fame of Emily Dickinson and her strange, strong poems.

To the geologist, ten thousand years seem but a step. From evidences about Amherst and Northampton he assigns this length of time, "one of the shortest estimates," as the probable interval since the glacial period. In that age, misty and remote enough to the layman, the ice, covering all this region, furrowed deeply into the sandstone, particularly north of the Holyoke range, largely forming its bold and rugged outline; it piled together other masses into rough hills, leaving in its path bowlders and clay and the stony soil so characteristic of New England.

When this mass of ice, beginning to yield to the oncoming of a more genial age, melted in the sun, a great lake was formed, whose height was three hundred feet above the sea, and two hundred feet above present low water in the Connecticut River. Its shores were the present boundaries of the valley. The surface of the ground over which we drive in the mellow August weather, listening to the peaceful farming sounds on every hand, was the actual bottom of this great prehistoric lake, in whose clays an abundant glacial flora has been found.

There is evidence that the lake speedily shrunk to almost the present size of the river. This "Nile of New England" has gradually deposited the rich alluvial meadows, its chief wealth and beauty.

Swinging through past centuries in other curves than now, it has formed seven great "ox-bows," cutting off subsequently all but the famous one, so distinctly seen from the summit of Mount Holyoke. Two of the others are found to have disappeared only since the settlement of the valley. Three of the seven were in Hatfield, and four in Northampton.

Ages before even the oncoming of the ice period, earthquakes and volcanic explosions carved our valley into a semblance of its present shape. Filled with waters from the sea, a narrow inlet or fjord to a height above the level of Mount Holyoke, it endured through triassic times.

Streams sweeping into the basin deposited sand and gravel flats. In these mud shores, animals long extinct and unimaginable made a huge procession of footprints since hardened into stone. These have been discovered, preserved, and described by the late President Hitchcock of Amherst College. Traces of reptiles, insects, fishes, and colossal frogs are here found, and also the enormous prints of birds whose size, to correspond with their tracks, must have been at least five times that of the ostrich. These bird-tracks occur in thirty places through the Connecticut Valley, between the upper strata. Into the late discussions of whether these great creatures with feet eighteen or twenty inches long were birds or not rather some unknown, three-toed animal we cannot enter. It is for us enough to know that the stupendous procession has been made to live again by the untiring genius of an enthusiast to whom we owe the resurrection of a long-vanished past; and bird or animal, "strange indeed, is this menagerie of remote sandstone days."

From this weird occupancy of antediluvian monsters to the days when the Agawams and other Indian tribes lived their nomadic and warlike lives in the fair vale, is a long step for a tense imagination.

Here, however, they were found; for how many years they had been here, or whence their pioneers may have come, cannot be certainly proven. But in 1631 the Connecticut first became known to our own forefathers. Early in the autumn of 1633 four men from Dorchester first visited its banks. Later, William Pynchon and his little band of followers, chiefly planters from Roxbury, came by the famous "Bay Path" through a hundred miles of forest to what is now the city of Springfield.[26]

An absorbing piety characterized these early settlements, as it had the original ones on the coast; and a "meeting-house" was an earliest care. The first framed house was erected by Mr. Pynchon; and deeds for the various allotments of land, the first ever executed in Western Massachusetts, were drawn up whereby a formal purchase was secured from the Indians, who held from Nature herself a dateless and unwritten title.

In all the early settlements it is a pleasant reflection that these legitimate purchases were always made with the wild but original owners.

Northampton was subsequently settled, its rich meadow land proving very attractive. In 1654 measures were taken here also to build and establish a meeting-house. What means of calling the settlers together for worship may have been employed is not certainly known. While in Springfield this important instrument was a drum, it is believed that a large and sonorous cow-bell was first used in Northampton. Later, a salary is recorded as being paid for services in "blowing the trumpet," presumably for the same purpose.

In 1659 about fifty settlers established the town of Hadley, its magnificent street twenty rods wide still bearing evidence to the good taste and forethought of those who planned the village. The name of Hadley was not given until two years later. Here, as in the first two settlements, measures were not only promptly taken for establishing churches, but schools were equally early in the thought of its founders.

That this appreciation of education was inherent and vital is shown by the noble array of famous educational institutions along the Connecticut to-day. Mount Holyoke College,[27] Smith College,[28] Amherst College, the State Agricultural College, the schools at Northfield, summer schools in every direction, and a host of lesser institutions, are the blossoms of that early aspiration and endeavor.

So far, the terms of agreement with the Indians had been carefully kept; any complaints from them had received immediate attention and adjustment, and everything was peaceable and friendly. Notwithstanding this pleasant state of affairs, military companies were maintained against any possibility of danger, as well as fortified houses in every town.

In 1662 Hampshire County was established, chiefly unsettled territory. It was then much larger than now, for the entire counties of Worcester and Berkshire have since been taken from its original boundaries. Deerfield and Hatfield were settled in 1670, and Northfield in 1673. In these early days Amherst was a part of Hadley, and it was not laid out until 1703.

West Street in Hadley.

The early peacefulness of the relations between Indians and settlers in the valley seems to have been largely due to the just and considerate policy of William Pynchon. The outbreak of "King Philip's War," in 1675, put an end to this quiet comfort. With a plan which appeared to embrace the sweeping away of every settlement from the north down the river, Northfield was completely burned by Indians, Deerfield had fallen with the terrible massacre at Bloody Brook, and Hatfield, Hadley, and Northampton came next.[29] In the meantime, however, the natives about Springfield, spurred to emulation by the ghastly deeds in the north, had gathered there, and burned nearly everything except the fortified houses where the inhabitants had fled for safety.

In the first attack on Hatfield the skill of the English more than matched the numbers of their assailants.

In Northampton, also, they were repulsed, but only after severe loss and destruction.

Old Hadley is still full of the traditions of those early days. On the 12th of June, 1676, at least seven hundred Indians attacked Hadley. It was then and there that the famous stranger, noble in dress and manner, dignified and venerable, unable longer to remain an idle spectator of so terrible events, issued forth and assumed command of the English forces, directing them in the most skilfully military manner. Encouraging and rallying, now at one point, now at another, his is perhaps the most picturesque and impressive figure in all our early history.

By his aid the Indians were repulsed with slight loss to the English; and, this accomplished, the mysterious stranger disappeared as silently and suddenly as he came. With the superstition of the times, it is not surprising that he was devoutly believed to be an angel from heaven, sent to save the colony in a disastrous crisis.

It was afterward ascertained that this opportunely guardian angel was no other than Goffe, the regicide, who with his father-in-law, Whalley, and twenty-eight other judges, had been condemned in England for passing sentence of death upon Charles I., and had escaped in 1660.[30] Both Goffe and Whalley had been officers of high rank in Cromwell's army. Escaping after their sentence, they had found refuge in 1664 at Hadley, unknown to all its inhabitants save the family who sheltered them.

In 1678 a peace was concluded, and King Philip finally conquered.

Beauty in dress and the love of fine clothes did not perish entirely, even with a background of bloodshed and slaughter. We learn that in 1651 a law was passed in Massachusetts, restraining excess in dress. In 1673 twenty-five wives and five maids were tried before a jury for being persons of small estate, yet wearing silk against the law.

A year later the wife of a Hadley man was again presented for wearing silk. She was found guilty, and fined ten shillings.

At the March court in 1676 sixty-eight persons were presented by the jury, among them thirty young men, "some for wearing silk, and that in a flaunting manner, and others for long hair and other extravagances."

Witchcraft seems not to have flourished in this rich and verdant valley, particularly in Hampshire County, to the extent which prevailed in the earlier settlements on the rocky coast. In 1645 the first cases of witchcraft in New England occurred at Springfield. During King Philip's War it lay dormant, naturally, under the more exciting events about.

But at the close of the war it revived; and a remarkable instance occurred at Hadley, when a Mr. Philip Smith was believed to be beset by the spells of a wretched old woman, who caused all sorts of mysterious evils to assail him, finally causing his death. The old woman, however, was allowed to live on; and there is no evidence of her ever having been brought to trial. About the time that Amherst was being laid out as one of the "precincts" of Hadley, fresh disasters awaited the valley dwellers, whose whole early progress seems to have been one long record of struggles with every sort of trial and discouragement.

The brave settlement at Deerfield again became the scene of bloodshed and cruelty, when, at the beginning of Queen Anne's War, the French and Indians descended upon it, murdering and torturing on every hand.[31] The famous Deerfield bell was taken during this campaign, and is believed to be still hanging in a little mission church on the St. Lawrence River.

The long-suffering valley dwellers were alternately allowed to breathe freely for a time, and then made to suffer all the distress of repeated wars for an almost endless succession of years. But in 1760, permanent peace came about, upon the surrender of the Canadian province to Great Britain.

For nearly one hundred and thirty years wars had racked Western Massachusetts to its foundations.

Hardly an acre of the beautiful green Connecticut Valley, now full of peace and sunshine and homely sound of toil, but has known the pressure of flying feet, hard-pressed by savage pursuer,—but has echoed to the terrible shouts of slayer and victim, or has drunk the blood of friends and foes.

And yet even these events faded into the dim past before the oncoming excitements of the Revolution.

Few events of particular significance at this crisis occurred in the Connecticut Valley itself, although its roll of minute-men is a long and honorable one. There were, however, many famous representatives of Toryism in the region.

The only event of local interest in this general connection was the "Shays' Rebellion," practically an uprising owing to a petulant feeling on the part of the insurgents that they had not been getting their full dues in various ways. Headed by Daniel Shays of Shutesbury, they marched against Springfield and threatened the courts and the arsenal.[32] There was little bloodshed, and the chief indirect effect of the rebellion was to hasten the adoption of a Federal government.

A camping ground is still pointed out northeast of Amherst.

From the close of this rebellion onward, life prospered in the valley. Amherst, and its neighboring towns, strongly disapproved, and publicly expressed its disapproval, of the War of 1812, being then, apparently, as ever, rather upon the conservative than the impetuous side of life.

The primitive means of crossing the Connecticut River were, of course, ferries, for it does not appear certain that at any points between New Hampshire and Connecticut were available fords. In May, 1718, nine pounds were raised for a free ferry for a year. The navigation of the Connecticut had always been a difficult problem, owing to the falls at South Hadley and Montague. It was not until after the close of the Revolution, and of Shays' Rebellion, which had for twelve years occupied the minds of all in Western Massachusetts, that an enterprise for facilitating transportation sprang into new life. This was the building of canals around these falls. In 1792 this laudable enterprise was authorized by the legislature, and the names of those forming the corporation are still preserved.

For many years the bridging of the Connecticut, or "Great River," was considered an impossible feat. It was attempted in 1792 at Greenfield. A toll-bridge was established at Springfield about 1805. It was over twelve hundred feet long, and built with six imposing arches. Its opening to the public was an occasion of great rejoicing, processions, and speeches.

The two travellers, whose glance backward over the long history of the fertile region they were passing so happily through had filled the whole golden afternoon, were now approaching the primitive and picturesque ferry at North Hadley. They hailed the sturdy boatman, who took them slowly across to the lovely Hatfield shore by hand. An idyllic little trip.

In these August afternoons the sun begins to lean toward the horizon by six o'clock. A fresh coolness, even after the hottest days, springs into the air, and the two in the carriage passed herds of cows, soft-eyed and gentle, on their homeward way from pasture.

As the level sun-rays swept across the meadows, the green of the rich grass was turned into velvety softness. The far, faint hills in the west came forth in a deep purple evening dress. While yet it seemed to be summer, an unsuspected scarlet leaf of sumac glowed suddenly by the roadside,—brilliant forerunner of that palpitating glory of color which holds high carnival here throughout a royal autumn.

In this calm time how remotely misty seem those volcanic days when all was but a strife of upheaval,—how impossible the stupendous procession of prehistoric mammoths who left their huge footprints in the mud of that perpetual summer,—how equally far away the numb clasp of the glacial silence,—how more than strange the knowledge that the bed of a great lake makes now the fertile farm, the shady woodland, the radiant roadside!

Nearer, yet still remote, the war-cries and the tragedies of two hundred and fifty years ago, and the sturdy strength and inflexibility of purpose which built up and made possible the beautiful life we know to-day.

As the cool twilight descends, and one dwelling after another is passed, the little home lights flash out cheerily into the still evening.

The warm yellow glow in the west grows less; one bright star, sentinel outpost of a countless host, springs into life, and all the sweet valley sleeps under the sky.

## Chapter 3

# A Few Delightful Drives

In all New England there are few regions offering more delightful opportunities for riding and driving than the portion of the Connecticut Valley in which the town of Amherst lies. For miles around, easy country roads wind along the highlands and through the valleys, displaying lavishly all the beauty and grandeur of which indulgent Nature is capable. It is like a vast park, through which one may wander for months without exhausting the natural attractions, and be more deeply impressed each day by the wonderful variety. Not a few are the visitors who come to Amherst, and some of the neighboring towns, expressly to spend an outing in driving; and none depart disappointed.

With Amherst as a centre, there are long drives of a day or more to Pittsfield and Lenox, fashionable as summer and fall resorts; to Worthington and Peru, on the lower Green Mountains, directly westward from Amherst, and twelve hundred and sixteen hundred feet above sea-level; between Goshen and Ashfield—both delightful places in themselves—is a charming "Little Switzerland"; and, further to the west, Williamstown and the Berkshire Hills are prominent; Brattleboro' and Burlington are the pleasant objective points in Vermont, as are Monadnock in New Hampshire and Wachusett in Massachusetts. Indeed, the list is almost limitless. Of the shorter and more important drives for those who visit Amherst to become acquainted with the town and its surroundings, a few of the best have been selected for brief mention in this book.

The ride to Mount Holyoke, eight miles, takes one to an outlook not surpassed in the world. The road runs southeasterly to the Middle Street of Hadley, four miles; then south, along the Connecticut River, two and one-half miles, with many choice views; then up the mountainside through the veil of the old forest to the half-way house. The rest of the trip to the summit is made in a quaint little car holding four persons, and making the ascent under a covered way by means of a stationary engine at the bottom. Athletes will prefer to climb the 522 steps which follow the side of the railway. Since the opening of the railroad in 1854, there has never been an accident. The summit has a perpendicular elevation of 954 feet, and from it may be seen four States and forty towns, eight of which are in Connecticut. The panorama of the winding river, fertile valley, and rugged mountains, as far as the eye can see, well nigh defies description. The drive home may be varied by crossing the Hockanum ferry at the foot of the mountain, and following the other side of the river to Northampton, and thence to Amherst.

Mount Holyoke.

"Old" Hadley, four miles, by the "old road," Amity Street, or by Northampton Street. The cemetery, the broad streets lined with elms, and the Elmwood House, are the objects of interest. The latter is on the site of the house where, two hundred years ago, Rev. Mr. Russell, the first minister of the town, hid the regicide judges, Goffe and Whalley, who had fled from England at the fall of Cromwell. From this hidingplace Goffe emerged to assume command of the settlers and drive off the attacking Indians in a memorable battle.

The "Meadow City," as Northampton is known, is an eight-mile drive over a straight road.[33] It is a thriving young city of fifteen thousand inhabitants, and many busy mills of almost national repute.[34] It has been the home of such men as the Rev. Jonathan Edwards, Governor Caleb Strong, Rev. Timothy Dwight, and to-day numbers among its inhabitants the noted novelist George W. Cable, Judge D.W. Bond, and President L. Clark Seelye. Northampton has many charming drives within its limits. Round Hill affords extensive views of river and meadow, and is of interest because of its connection with the historians Bancroft and Motley, and the "sweet singer," Jenny Lind. "Paradise" is a delightful bit of nature preserved from the ruthless real estate agent by kindly hands. One may reach it for a walk from Paradise road. Among the other objects of interest in the city are Smith College for young ladies, the Clark Institute for deaf and dumb, and the many manufactories. Wade, Warner & Co., the publishers of "Picturesque Hampshire," and projectors of similar works of other Western Massachusetts counties, have a large printing business here, and publish the Hampshire County Journal, a prominent weekly.

Florence, three miles beyond Smith College, is the terminus of the horse-car line. A drive through it to Leeds, one and a half miles, and then along the stream to Haydenville and Williamsburg, brings one to the scene of the Mill River disaster of 1874, when 158 lives were destroyed in less than an hour.[35] These towns are pleasant manufacturing villages.

Easthampton, eleven miles, by way of Northampton, is the seat of Williston Academy, a well-known preparatory school for boys. Returning by way of Mount Tom station and the Hockanum ferry lengthens the distance to fourteen miles.

Mount Nonatuck, on the opposite side of the river from Mount Holyoke, is ten miles from Amherst, whether one crosses the Connecticut by the Hockanum ferry, or goes by way of Northampton, and the meadow road to the south. The ascent is by a carriage road, to the top, 852 feet above sea-level, where there is a comfortable house. The view from the summit is scarcely less beautiful than from Mount Holyoke.

PLAINVILLE; two miles; a little settlement in the town of Hadley; Amity Street, first right after descending the hill. From Plainville thence by first left, around the base of Mount Warner, to North Hadley, and return by the northern side of the mountain, is a pleasant drive of nine miles.

The HUNTINGTON ESTATE; three and a half miles; Amity Street River, then following the river north directly west ward. The first large house at the left is the summer home of Bishop F.D. Huntington, and with the adjoining estates is a fine example of the older Connecticut Valley homesteads. Following the river, the return may be made by North Hadley.

HATFIELD is five miles by way of North Hadley, and across the river by a picturesque ferry. This town was one of the earliest of those settled in this portion of the valley, and its history is filled with accounts of Indian wars. It is laid out in two long streets, lined from end to end with magnificent elms and pleasant estates. The return, if by way of Northampton, southward, is eleven miles; or by Sunderland, northward, is fourteen miles, either way of great variety and charm.

WHATELY and WHATELY GLEN; twelve miles; is a delightful picnicking spot, and a haunt of artists and lovers of nature. North Hadley, the ferry to Hatfield, and northwesterly roads from Hatfield Centre. The return may be made by Sunderland, a mile or two further.

NORTH AMHERST; two miles; North Pleasant Street. Return may be made by taking road to the west, to North Hadley, thence southeasterly to Amherst, the whole distance being from nine to twelve miles, according to variations; or by the easterly road to North Amherst "city"; whole distance five miles. North Amherst "city" is two miles from Amherst by way of Mount Pleasant Street.

MOUNT TOBY is eight miles due north through North Amherst and the Leverett plain, into wildness where bowlders, hugh forest trees, clearest springs and brooks surround an unequalled bit of rural loveliness, at the very base of the mountain. A climb of two miles by an easy mountain road brings one to the top. From the wooden tower, now destroyed by fire, could once be seen a wild sea of mountain tops and lands in more than eighty towns.

It is seven miles to SHUTESBURY by way of North Amherst "city," and following along the side of the roaring waters of the upper Mill River. The road is picturesque, and at times shut in as if there were no outside world; but from the crest, with a deep chasm farther east, one can look far over valley, hill, and range, and see Greylock in the west, Monadnock in the north, and Wachusett in the east.

LEVERETT, six miles, through North Amherst "city," and directly north, affords a fine series of views. A pleasant way is by way of North Amherst and Factory Hollow.

LOCK'S PONDS, in North Leverett; twelve miles; a pleasant place to picnic.

MONTAGUE, ten miles, through North Amherst, north through Leverett, passing Mount Toby, is a wide and picturesque drive.

SUNDERLAND, seven miles, through North Amherst, directly north.[36]

To reach SOUTH DEERFIELD by way of the Sunderland bridge, one must go through North Amherst village in a northwesterly direction for ten miles, passing through the villages of North Amherst and Sunderland. Sugar Loaf Mountain, around whose base the road winds, after crossing the bridge, is well worth ascending.[37] The town of Old Deerfield, five miles farther, is of great historical interest, and in it are many memorials of the fierce French and Indian wars that more than once devastated it. The return drive may be made through the North Hatfield meadows, directly south, and across the river by the Hatfield ferry, and thence to Amherst.

In PELHAM the fishing-rod factory of the Montague City Rod Company is an interesting place to visit. It is about two miles directly east from Main Street. This industry was founded in the year 1860 by H. Gray & Son; and was the first factory known in which fishing-rods were made by machinery. The founders carried on a constantly increasing business for fourteen years, and in 1874 sold out to J.U. Ward & Co.

This firm continued until 1880, when the business passed into the hands of Bartlett Brothers. The senior member of this firm, L.L. Bartlett, withdrew in 1883, and E.P. Bartlett, sole proprietor during the next six years, greatly enlarged the plant, and trebled the amount of business.

In 1889 the business combined with the Montague City Rod Company. This company now employs at this factory a full force of fifty hands, and has a constantly increasing business.[38] Their annual output is about six thousand fishing-rods of all grades, ranging from the boys' cheap rod to the finest German silver mounted split bamboo rods. The catalogue contains descriptions of the two hundred different styles of fishing-rods manufactured. The stock used is the native ash, maple, and

Fishing rod factory at Pelham.

birch; also lancewood and greenheart wood imported from the West Indies, and bamboo poles from Calcutta. Mr. E.P. Bartlett, who is now in charge at this factory, has been connected with the business ever since it started, and as either part or sole owner during the last seventeen years. It is owing in a large measure to his energy and business capacity that the business has grown and developed to its present large volume. His enterprise has aided very materially in the growth of the manufacturing interest of Amherst. The Montague City Rod Company has another large factory for fishing-rods at Montague City. The officers of the company are President, L.L. Bartlett of Montague City; treasurer, C.W. Hazelton of Turner's Falls. E.P. Bartlett is one of the directors of the company, and superintendent of the factory at Pelham. Amherst is the post-office address of this branch of the firm.

West Pelham church; four miles; and thence southward, behind the first mountain range following a mad brook down to Pansy Park, is a pleasant drive. The way is about fifteen miles if the return to Amherst is by going southeasterly to the Bay road, and thence through South Amherst.

The tower on Mount Lincoln is six miles due east to the West Pelham meeting-house, and thence south, clinging to the left-hand roads with guide-boards. The roads follow a deep chasm at the left, a private graveyard at the right, the mountain woods, and along the mountain top to the summit. The tower is twelve hundred feet above the sea-level, the surrounding valleys, and no other point gives a clearer idea of the Connecticut Valley as a whole. As the position is higher than Mounts Holyoke and Tom and the Sugar Loaves, one may look directly across them to the distant and loftier continuations of the Green Mountains.

Pratt's Corner; four to six miles, according to the variations; East Street, turning north, and taking the first road to the northeast. This way is along the valley of the Pelham hills, and full of most charming scenery.

Pansy Park, the flower farm and seed establishment of L.W. Goodell, is situated about four miles from Amherst, upon the main road to Belchertown, and about a mile this side of the railroad station, which takes its name from this place. Here in the summer time may be seen more than two thousand varieties of flowering plants, including pansies, asters, pinks, petunias, and many others, being grown by the acre for the seed. Especially during the months of August and September, all these make a gorgeous display of floral beauty, which attracts thousands of visitors annually from far and near. One of the most attractive features of the place is the aquatic garden and artificial pond, containing one of the largest collections of water-plants grown in the open air in America. Among other rarities in this collection are several varieties of the Japanese and sacred Egyptian lotus, and about twenty varieties of water-lilies from various parts of the world, including the magnificent blue and red lilies from Zanzibar. The cultivation of the latter has until recently been confined to the city parks and the grounds of the wealthy, on account of the high price of the plants; but Mr. Goodell has shown that they can be as easily grown from the seed as the common annuals, and made to flower in tubs, and in this way they are now being grown from seed he has distributed all over the country. The very rare Victoria Regia, from the river Amazon, the largest water-lily in the world, with leaves from four to

A specimen of Victoria Regia, the largest water lily in the world, grown at Pansy Park.

six feet across, was flowered at Pansy Park in the summer of 1890 without artificial heat, the first time this has ever been accomplished in an open pond. The taste for the cultivation of aquatic plants increased so rapidly that the following season Mr. Goodell constructed ponds to cover several acres, and is cultivating this class of plants on a larger scale than has ever before been attempted. In addition to the seeds grown upon the farm, large quantities are imported from the growers of England, Germany, and France, and some varieties that require a long season to mature are grown on contract in the Southern States. A catalogue and price list is published annually in January by Mr. Goodell, and thousands of them sent out.[39] The seeds are put up in hundreds of thousands of packets, and go by mail or express to customers in all parts of the country, and in fact all over the globe, as orders are received from Europe, the East and the West Indies, Japan, Australia, New Zealand, and other foreign lands. Mr. Goodell's success in a business started under discouraging circumstances, and in competition with old established firms, is remarkable. He began during the Centennial year, with a capital of only $25, on a poor, run-down farm, which was mortgaged and otherwise deeply in debt. The old homestead, which has been in the Goodell family for over a century, was a few years ago one of the most neglected and unsightly in town, and would in the ordinary course of events have become one of the much-talked-of "abandoned farms." It is now a most attractive place, and well worth a long journey to visit. The year Mr. Goodell began business, he had less than two hundred customers, while now there are over fifty thousand. From two hundred to five hundred orders are received daily during the selling season in the winter and spring months. Six years ago, land more suitable for the cultivation of the flowers being needed, Mr. Goodell bought the two estates adjoining his own, where most of the growing has been done. Pansies being one of the leading specialties, the distinctive name of "Pansy Park" was then given to the place.

A view of the Belchertown Common.

BELCHERTOWN; ten miles; a pleasant village on the hills at the southeast. The road is direct after passing through the East Amherst village and by the Agricultural Fair grounds. Good hotel accommodations, with several summer residences and a handsome library building, add to the natural attractiveness of the place. A half a mile beyond the Pansy Park Station of the Massachusetts Central Railroad, the road passes the site of the birthplace of Dr. J.G. Holland, the well-remembered author.[40] In the grove, at the right, just before crossing the railroad at Pansy Park Station, there was formerly a school-house in which Henry Ward Beecher, when a student at Amherst College, preached his first sermon. Beautiful roads and picnic grounds about the ponds abound between Amherst and Belchertown. The drive from Belchertown to Enfield offers land views of more than ordinary loveliness.[41]

SOUTH AMHERST; four miles; South Pleasant Street, following the left-hand road after ascending the hill beyond Mill River.

The OLD BAY ROAD; four miles; the right-hand road after ascending the hill beyond Mill River, once the southern boundary of the town. It runs along the foot of the Holyoke range, was first a bridle-path, and later a part of the stage route between Northampton, Hadley, Brookfield, and Boston. The "Bay Path" has been made memorable by Dr. Holland. The road commands an immense variety of landscape.

The NOTCH; five miles; to the Bay road, thence over the Holyoke Mountain range. This cut was the first outlet of the great lake which once spread over this portion of the Connecticut Valley.

South Hadley and Granby, each eight miles, are beyond the Notch. The former place is the seat of the Mount Holyoke College for young ladies, a well-known educational institution. Returning home by the road around the base of Mount Holyoke will give variety, and add only three miles to the distance. By crossing Smith's Ferry in South Hadley, the only ferry on the river which is operated by the force of the current, and following the river to Northampton, the drive will be lengthened by five miles. Granby is a small town, in early times a portion of Hadley.

Chapter 4

# Amherst of the Present

The town of Amherst occupies a position a little east of the centre of Hampshire County, which was established by act of the General Court, May 7, 1662. The original county included the present Berkshire County, set off in 1761; Franklin County, set off in 1811; and Hampden County, set off in 1812. There is but one city in Hampshire County, Northampton, and of the twenty-two towns, Amherst is the second in point of population. The total population of the county, according to the national census of 1890, was 51,859.

Adjoining Amherst are: Sunderland and Leverett, in Franklin County, on the north; Shutesbury, in Franklin County, Pelham, and Belchertown, on the east; Granby, on the south; and Hadley, on the west. On two sides, nature has provided the town sharp boundary lines in the ranges of the Pelham hills and Holyoke mountains.

Between these and the highlands, where the main village lies, intervene broad valleys, which stretch away westward, to the banks of the peaceful river. Several minor streams traverse the town in their journey to the Connecticut, here and there broadening into graceful ponds, which never fail to attract the migrating water-fowl in spring and fall, affording many a good shot to the chance sportsman. The woods and the brooks as well furnish in their seasons similar amusement, although the latter are fast becoming desolated. The whirr of the partridge, the chatter of the squirrel, and the bobbing white tail of the rabbit, frequently startle the wandering scholar who loves to give himself to solitude and communion with nature. Sometimes a very shrewd hunter is permitted to hear and see these things, if he is careful to be unarmed.

The area of Amherst is about twenty-eight and three-quarters square miles, and its villages are Amherst, North Amherst, North Amherst "city," East Amherst, or East Street, and South Amherst.

The distances from the centre to the surrounding villages are: North Amherst and the "city," two miles; East Amherst, one mile; South Amherst, four miles. North Amherst "city" is a mile eastward from North Amherst.

The roads and streets that connect these villages with each other and with the neighboring towns are, in the main, the smoothest and most comfortable of country thoroughfares. Within the limits of constant and heavy travel they are laid and kept in repair with a thoroughness seldom seen in towns of equal size. Their entire length is about seventy-five miles.

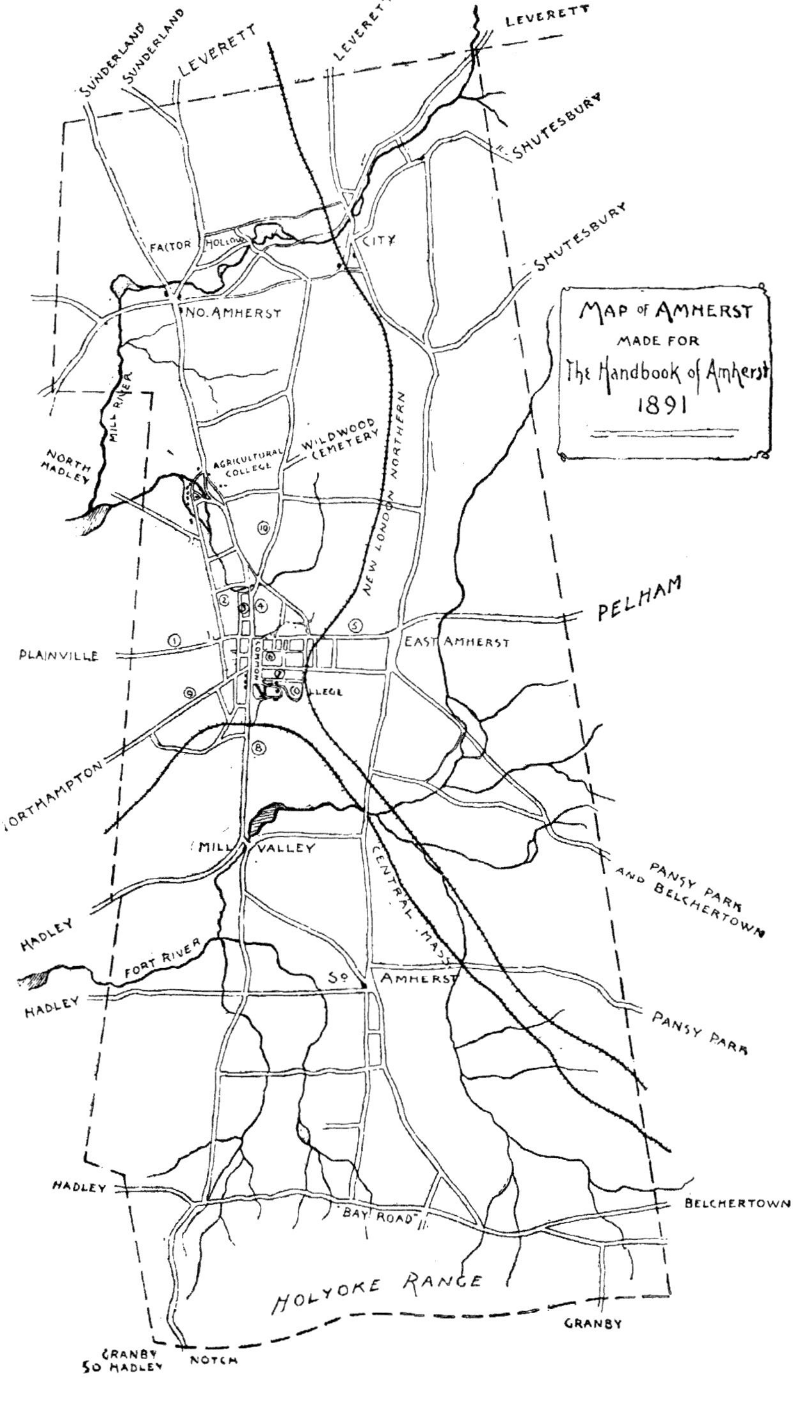


Map of Amherst, 1891.

The New London Northern Railroad has stations at South Amherst, Amherst, and North Amherst "city." The distance from New London, Conn., where the road connects with the New York, Providence, and Boston and the New York, New Haven and Hartford Railroads, and with the steamer for New York, to Amherst is 85 miles; from Willimantic, connecting with the New York and New England road, 56 miles; from Palmer, connecting with the Boston and Albany, 20 miles; from Belchertown, connecting with the Massachusetts Central, 10 miles; from Brattleboro, connecting with the Connecticut River, and the Central Vermont, 36 miles; and from Miller's Falls, connecting with the Fitchburg, 15 miles.

The Massachusetts Central Railroad was extended through Amherst in 1888, and has stations at South Amherst and Amherst.[42] Boston is 96 miles distant; Oakdale, where connections are made with the Worcester and Nashua Railroad, 55 miles; Belchertown, connecting with the New London Northern, 9 miles; and Northampton, connecting with the Connecticut River and the New York, New Haven and Hartford roads, 8 miles.

In politics, Amherst is usually found within the Republican fold. Its local elections are not carried on strongly marked political lines, but they are frequently more exciting than the State or national contests.[43] There are about one thousand voters.

A few statistics will give the practical reader an idea of the material conditions of the town. The tax rate for the year 1890 was $15.75 on every $1,000, and during the four years previous averaged $15.50. In comparing this rate with that of other towns, the discount of ten per cent allowed in return for early payments must be taken into consideration.

Law and order have an almost undisputed sway over Amherst, and the guardians of the peace are limited to a dozen constables and one night patrolman. The grounds of the two colleges are protected by specially appointed watchmen. The town lock-up is with rare exceptions desolate of inmates. It frequently shelters a weary tramp from the cold, but offenders against the law, scarcely at the rate of a half-dozen a year.

The fire department consists of two hose companies and a hook and ladder company, all under the charge of a board of twelve engineers appointed by the selectmen. In 1891 thirty-eight men comprised the working force of firemen. Hydrants are located at convenient intervals in the thickly settled portions of the town, and the force of the water supply is such that the hand-engine is seldom called into service. In the past four years, since 1887, the average number of fires has been five.

The main village of Amherst is lighted by gas and electricity.

A water system was introduced by a private company in 1881, supplying all the main portions of the town. The source of the supply is Amethyst Brook, four miles distant, in Pelham, and chemical examination has shown the water to be of excellent purity.

Shortly after the introduction of water, a sewerage system was planned by the several influential citizens, and put in at the expense of benefiting abutters. It now consists of three divisions emptying into running brooks in different parts of the village, and the service is sufficient for the accommodation of all living in this portion of the town.

The Amherst Common, looking toward Amherst College.

One of the most attractive features of the village of Amherst is the Common, a long stretch of greensward reaching from the Amherst College buildings to the business blocks. Previous to 1880 it was an unsightly swamp, and was changed to its present good condition through the efforts of William A. Dickinson, Esq. The expenses were defrayed by private subscription, and at present it is largely cared for by the local improvement society.

The national census of 1890 placed the population of Amherst at 4,512,—an increase of 214 in ten years. As augmenting the social and business life of the town, the 500 students attending the two colleges may well be added to this number. The actual growth of the town may be readily seen from these census figures: In 1776 there were 915 inhabitants; 1790, 1,233; 1800, 1,358; 1810, 1,469; 1820, 1,917; 1830, 2,631; 1840, 2,550; 1850, 3,057; 1860, 3,206; 1870, 4,035; 1880, 4,298.

The elevated situation, the pure air from the hills, the excellent water supply, and the freedom of a country life, combined with the material comforts of modern homes, make Amherst one of the healthiest and most cheerful of the towns of Western Massachusetts. The deaths average about sixty-five in a year, and the proportion of sickness is small.

Amherst exults in still retaining that ancient emblem of pure democracy, the town-meeting, and many are the patriotic words, sage counsels, and, it must be confessed, now and then, bits of oratorical filling, that have echoed in the ears of the oldest inhabitants at these assemblages of the people. The college boys have always been zealous in their attendance upon town-meetings, and there is more than one legend among them of the absurdities that were gravely legislated upon in the mythical times when students are said to have been allowed to cast their votes on important town matters. If such times ever did exist, no one can clearly remember them, although of course this casts no doubt upon the truth of these circulating stories. The annual meeting, when officers are elected and appropriations made, occurs on the first Monday in March.

The yearly expenditures of the town reach about $42,000. In 1890 they were $110,947, which included the cost of the new town hall. The public debt in that year was $142,000. The total valuation of taxable property was $3,290,128. About $2,000,000 is untaxable. The taxable personal property amounted to $931,314, and real estate $2,358,814.

The educational interests of Amherst are well provided for in the annual appropriations. The schools in 1891 were eleven in number, with twenty-one regular teachers. The expenditures for schools in the year 1890-91 were $11,499, or $14 for every pupil. The school buildings and land are valued at about $60,000. Amherst schools rank well among those of the State. One of the three committeemen is usually the superintendent.

The village of Amherst is the business centre of the town. Three short brick blocks, wherein are located the majority of the stores of the town, radiate from the Amherst House, a hostelry bearing an enviable reputation throughout the State. For many years this site has been occupied by the hotel of the town. The original building was burned, with the rest of the blocks in Merchants' Row, in 1879. The present house was built directly after the fire, and is owned by the Conkey heirs. Ordinarily, one hundred guests may be accommodated, and at such occasions as the commencement of the colleges, special arrangements nearly double this capacity. Lorenzo Chase has been the proprietor since 1890. Connected with the hotel, T.L. Paige has a finely equipped livery stable.

About this end of the village Common are clustered the post-office, town hall, banks, newspaper office, and stores. At the further end rises College Hill, with its group of college buildings.

The Amherst House.

The village post-office and the Amherst Savings Bank are located in the block next the hotel. The employees of the post-office handle about 1,000,000 letters and 580,000 papers in a single year, and the cash receipts are never far from $10,000 a year.

The Savings Bank was incorporated April 15, 1864, and began business the 2d of January following. The amount of deposits, January 1, 1891, was $1,359,419. E.F. Cook was then president.

The comfortable quarters of the Amherst Club are in the next block, which belongs to B.H. Williams. This club was organized in 1891 by the young business men of the town, and it has handsomely appointed reception, reading, and billiard rooms. Herbert T. Cowles was the first president.[44]

The Amherst National Bank, in Hunt's Block, was organized in January, 1864, largely through the influence of the late Leonard M. Hills, who became its first president. At Mr. Hills' death, L.D. Hills succeeded to the office, which he has since held. The capital of the bank is $150,000.

The Baptist church stood for many years next to Hunt's Block. The society was organized as a branch of the New Salem and Prescott church, November 8, 1827, later becoming a branch of the church at Northampton, and recognized as an independent organization on August 3, 1832. This building was erected in 1855. The pastor in 1891 was Rev. J.B. Child.

Across the Common, on the corner of Spring Street, is the Grace Episcopal church, a handsome gray-stone structure, with a curious finger-like spire at one corner of the tower. The Right Reverend F.D. Huntington, Bishop of Central New York, organized the society, with thirty-seven members, September 12, 1864. Rev. S.P. Parker, D.D., was installed as the first pastor, January 11, 1865, and until March of the year following, services were held in the hall of the old Amherst Academy building, then standing on the present site of the Amity Street Grammar School. The church building was consecrated July 17, 1866: it cost $40,000, and has a seating capacity of five hundred. At present there is a generous active membership, and since 1888 the Rev. William J. Tilley has been the rector.

The town hall is a picturesque building of brick, red sandstone, and granite. It was erected by the town in 1889 at a cost of $58,000, H.S. McKay of Boston being the designer. In addition to a handsome hall, seating eight hundred and fifty persons, there are rooms for the town officers, the district court, the town library, and several business men.

In the rear of this hall, Company K, 2nd Regiment, M.V.M., has a large armory, built by the town in 1890 and rented to the State. The company was organized November 19, 1887, and in 1891 had full ranks with E.G. Thayer, captain; W.A. Thayer, 1st lieutenant; F.A. Bardwell, 2d lieutenant. W.G. Towne was the first captain.

In the rear of the American House Block, opposite, is the office of the *Amherst Record,* a thriving weekly, boasting its forty-eighth volume. It first appeared in 1844 under the name of the *Hampshire and Franklin Express,* Samuel C. Nash being editor. In 1865 it became the *Hampshire Express,* and three years later, the *Amherst Record. The Record* is published every Wednesday afternoon, and its editors, Carpenter & Morehouse, are the proprietors of a large job and book printing business.[45]

*Left*: Grace Episcopal Church.

*Below*: The Town Hall.

Kellogg's Block, at this end of the Phoenix Row, stands upon the site of the home of Noah Webster, who resided in Amherst from 1812 to 1822. The house was destroyed by fire in 1838.

Masonic Hall, in Cook's Block, is the headquarters of the Pacific Lodge of Masons, the E.M. Stanton Post 147, of the Grand Army, and the Women's Relief Corps.

It is a peculiarity of the village, that the chief streets radiate in every direction from the Common. The most satisfactory results, therefore, of an attempt to see whatever there is of interest, will be obtained by taking the Common as a starting-place for a walk through each one. They are not in any case thickly populated for more than a quarter of a mile from the Common, and a ramble about them, while not occupying a long time, will well repay an admirer of country scenery, in the sight of the many comfortable homes,—for Amherst is truly a village of homes,—and now and then the distant landscapes of rare beauty.

From the side of the Amherst House, Amity Street, the "old road" to Hadley, extends directly westward to the town boundary, Plainville, and the Connecticut River. It is the modern survivor of one of the original roads of the town, laid out with a width of forty rods in 1703.

The building opposite is a veritable landmark. When it was but one story high, it contained the town's first post-office, which was removed from East Amherst about 1820. The first postmaster sold out, after being a few years in this place, to one Jared White, who paid $100 for the business, and continued it in the same location. The building is now owned by Frank P. Wood, who opened it as Wood's Hotel in 1882. It is best known to the college boys as "Frank's," and the warm-hearted proprietor has had a permanent position in the usually fickle affections of the boys, ever since he first demonstrated to them his skill as a cook and his kindness as a friend. More than one class and club has celebrated their friendship for the man and the place in their publications, and many a delectable game bird, rare-bit, or lobster have they enjoyed during the days when the restaurant was open. "Frank" entered private life in 1889, but as a caterer he is still in great demand. His rooms are rented to college students.

The Grammar School building opposite stands upon the site of Amherst Academy, in its day the most prominent educational institution in this part of the State, and very influential in the founding of Amherst College.[46] Opened in December, 1814, the incorporators, when the charter was granted two years later, included all the leading citizens of the town, which was then about one-fourth its present population. For a dozen years both sexes were admitted to the Academy. A poor student preparing for the ministry was required to pay no tuition, and very frequently found kind people who gladly gave him his board. The number of pupils attending the Academy at one time amounted to ninety of each sex. After young ladies had been excluded, the number varied between seventy-five and one hundred. Connected with the Academy as a pupil was Mary Lyon, the founder of Mount Holyoke College at South Hadley. Among the teachers, since become prominent, was the venerable Professor William S. Tyler of Amherst College. The Academy building was a three-story brick structure, and being considered unsafe, was taken down in 1868 to make way for the present school-house.

"The Terrace"—a home "for backward and delicate children."

The old homestead of judge Strong, once the adjutant-general of Massachusetts, stands some distance back from the street. It is now owned by Mrs. S.E. Emerson.

At the opposite corner of North Pleasant Street is Mrs. R.G. Williams' Select Family School. The success of this institution and the experience of its teachers, who are Mrs. Williams, the Rev. Mr. Williams, and assistants, insure the most faithful and earnest instruction to the pupils.

Pleasantly situated on South Prospect Street, near Amity, is "The Terrace," Mrs. W.D. Herrick's Home School for backward and delicate children. Mrs. Herrick receives into her family a limited number of children, who, from disease or some untoward circumstance, are unfitted for the ordinary school. To these she devotes herself, faithfully aided by efficient and skilled teachers, who give to each pupil that care and training which the mental and physical peculiarities demand. The Home stands upon high ground, affording a commanding view of the beautiful Connecticut Valley and the Holyoke Mountain range, and it is perfect in its sanitary appointments. A fine lawn and ample playgrounds afford abundant opportunity for out-of-door exercise and recreation. The school has been established a number of years, and is favored with the confidence and patronage of the best physicians and educators of the country.

Among the other residences on Amity Street are those of Professor E.P. Crowell, Dean of Amherst College; E.B. Marsh, registrar of Amherst College; Professor Charles Wellington, Dr. Charles A. Goessmann, Professor CU. F. Mills, all of the Agricultural College, and the slimmer home of Hiram Heaton of New York. President H.H. Goodell of the Agricultural College lives on Sunset Avenue, near Amity.[47] On Lincoln Avenue, leading directly to the Agricultural College, is one of the finest views in the town. On this street is the house of Mrs. C.D. Adams.

That portion of Pleasant Street which extends northward from the hotel is most aptly named. For the distance of a quarter of a mile, great straight-trunked elms line each side of the road, almost uniting their branches overhead, and sheltering in the warm summer time many a tuneful katydid. The residences on the left side of the street are those of E.D. Bangs, the treasurer of the Savings Bank; the Conkey Mansion, now the parish home of St. Bridget's church, and occupied by the pastor, Rev. J.B. Drennan; the home of Levi Cowles, standing a generous distance back from the street; and the dwelling of George Cutler. On the other side, live W.H. Long, William Kellogg, whose house is on land bought from Noah Webster, and Dr. O.F. Bigelow. The Universalist Society, organized November, 1887, has a site for a church building here. The services are held in Masonic Hall, pending the erection of the church, and the Rev. J.H. Holden is pastor.

The village cemetery includes within its limits the graveyard that was laid out by the town of Hadley in 1830.

On the road toward the Agricultural College is the St. Bridget's Roman Catholic church, built in 1871. Previous to that time the Catholics of the town held their meetings in Palmer's Block, on the site of which the town hall now stands. Until 1872 the pastors came from Northampton, but in that year Rev. Francis Brennan was installed. The pastor since 1887, Rev. J.B. Drennan, is also pastor of the Hadley church. A short distance beyond is the residence of H.D. Fearing, manufacturer of straw hats. Leaving Pleasant Street here, it will be interesting to return to Mount Pleasant Street, which extends over the hills to North Amherst "city." A short distance from the fork of the two roads is Wildwood Cemetery, a most beautiful spot, bought and laid out in 1888 by a private corporation.

About a mile from the village, on the left of the road, is the Mount Pleasant House, of which Mrs. W.F. Bullman is the proprietor. The estate was formerly the property of Colonel W.S. Clark, president of the Agricultural College, and cost him nearly $40,000. The house stands upon the highest part of the hill, nearly four hundred feet above sea-level, and commands views of the Connecticut Valley that are limited only by the range of one's vision. It was after long travelling in foreign countries that Henry Ward Beecher stood here looking off upon the wide landscape, and said, "I have seen nothing finer in the world,"—a remark that has been repeated often by visitors of equal prominence. The extensive grounds of the estate, with its spacious lawns and shaded walks, are always models of the gardener's art.

Returning to the village square, a walk to the American House brings one to the corner of Lessey Street. The first two estates, on the left, belong to E.F. Cook, the president of the Savings Bank. The second of these is occupied by E.F. Cook, and the first by Lieutenant L.W. Cornish, military instructor at the Agricultural College. For many years, the Northampton and Amherst stages, owned by Mr. Cook, made their two daily trips from the stables in the rear of this house. At the completion of the railroad they were discontinued. The place is of historical interest, as it includes an orchard planted by Noah Webster.

Upon Oak Grove Hill, over which Lessey Street leads, are the residences of Rev. W.S. Tyler, D.D., of Amherst College, and his son, Professor J.M. Tyler. The house

Mount Pleasant House.

of Dr. Tyler was the birthplace and youthful home of Helen Hunt Jackson, whose writings, under the nom de-plume "H.H.," still charm many readers.

The Chapter houses of the Delta Kappa Epsilon fraternity are on the summit of the hill. The "Oak Grove School" for young ladies occupies the colonial mansion, formerly the residence of J. Howard Sweetser of New York, on the opposite side of the street. This school was founded in 1885, and is conducted by Miss V.W. Buffain, a graduate of Wellesley College, assisted by an able corps of instructors. The aim of the school is to train up girls with healthy bodies, sound minds, and refined manners. The facilities can hardly be excelled. The boarding pupils enjoy a well-kept home in a charming situation. Preparation is here made for college, several of the best institutions in the State accepting the certificates of the school in place of regular examinations for admission.

Main Street is a well-travelled thoroughfare along which one may look from the verandas of the Amherst House. It crosses New London Northern Railroad near the station, and extends through East Amherst to Pelham.

The meeting-house of the First Congregational Society, on the right side of the street, was dedicated September 23, 1868, the corner-stone having been laid September 21st of the previous year. The society dates back to the earliest settlement of the town, when there was no distinction between the religious and political body. The business of the parish was transacted in public meeting, and the necessary funds for its support were raised by taxation, together with those needed for highways and the other usual expenses of a town. The first meeting-house was built about 1840,

Oak Grove School.

upon the site of the present college Observatory. It was a severely plain structure without and within. Around the sides were ranged the pews, the men sitting on one side and the women on the other. The first minister was Rev. David Parsons. In 1788 a meeting-house of a more elaborate character was erected upon the same site, and three years after, private individuals contributed the money for the belfry. The opening of the College was followed by a need for better accommodations, and the third building, the present College Hall, was erected in 1829. This cost $6,500, and originally had a portico in front supported by huge pillars. When it was finished, the society decided that the town should hold no meetings in it, and it was after it had been occupied some years that the people became worldly enough to allow stoves, kerosene lights, and an organ to be admitted. The growth of the society since it has occupied the present building has been steady. It has now the largest membership in the town, excepting only the college church. The building cost $75,000. In the spring of 1890 the church celebrated its one hundred and fiftieth anniversary. Until July, 1891, Rev. G.S. Dickerman was pastor.

The residence of William A. Dickinson, Esq., treasurer of Amherst College, is situated upon the opposite side of the street. The estate adjoining has long been in the possession of the Dickinson family, and is now the home of Miss Lavinia Dickinson, whose sister, Emily Dickinson, left, at her death, the wonderful poems which have since been published and widely read. This house was the first brick building in Amherst.

The residence of the late Professor R.H. Mather is at the right. During the first year of his administration, President Gates occupied the house.

Further down the street, and standing some distance back, are the residences of Leonard D. Hills, president of the National Bank, and of Henry F. Hills, president of the Hills Company, manufacturers of straw goods.

*Above*: Main Street, Amherst.

*Below*: First Congregational Meeting House and Parsonage in 1788.

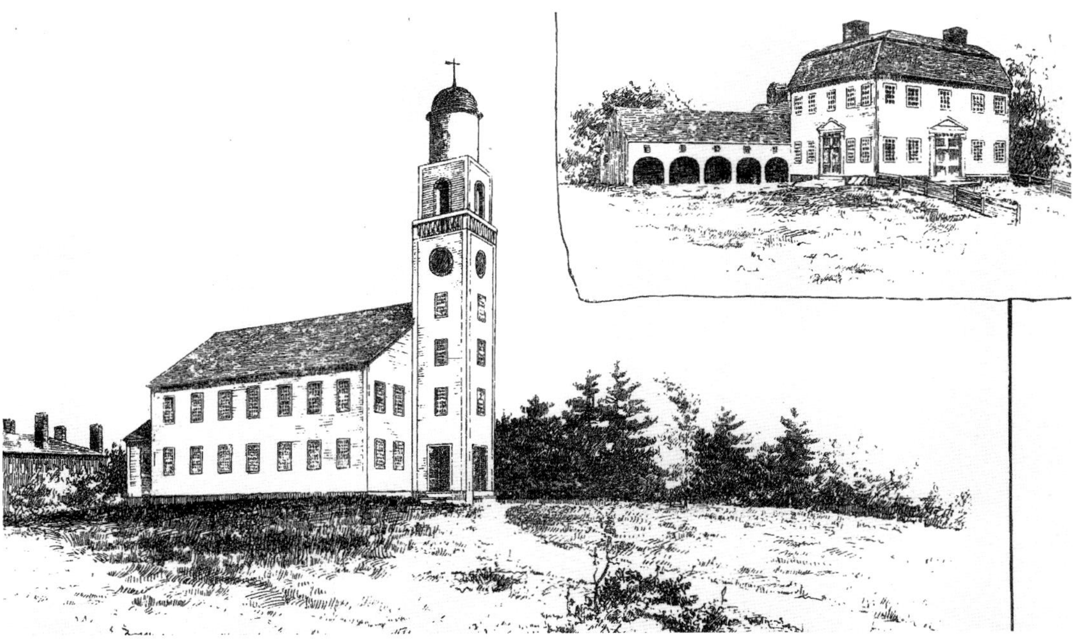

First Congregational Church.

Beyond the railroad, on the same street, is the church building of the Methodist Episcopal Society, first organized in 1868, with Rev. E.F. Pitcher, pastor, and reorganized in 1875, under Rev. S.L. Rogers. The present building was erected in 1879. In 1891 Rev. S.A. Bragg was the pastor.

The residence of S.A. Stevens is on the same side, near the East Street.

Grouped near the railroad station of the New London Northern road are the only manufactories of the village. The wooden buildings of The Hills Company are devoted to the manufacturing of straw goods. In the season closing May, 1891, this company made 350,000 dozen straw hats. H.D. Fearing & Co. occupy the brick building. Each year they turn out a large line of the finer grades of straw hats.

Spring Street, extending eastward from the centre of the village Common, has several pleasant residences, among them that of Professor D.P. Todd of Amherst College. The High School building, built about 1860, is here.

College Street is parallel with Spring Street. On the corner of the Common is the Beta Theta Pi House, and beyond, the Chi Phi and the Phi Delta Theta houses. The residences here include those of Dr. H.H. Seelye, assistant in the physical culture department of the Amherst College, Mrs. Laurens P. Hickok, widow of the late Dr. Hickok, whose works on philosophy perpetuate his name; Ex-President Julius H. Seelye, whose connection with Amherst College dates from 1855; Professor W.L. Montague, of Amherst College, and the director of the Summer School of Languages; Dr. Edward Hitchcock, son of the president of Amherst College of that name; Mrs. A.L Cooper; and Dr. T.P. Field.

On South Pleasant Street, beyond College Hill, are the Delta Upsilon House and the residence of Mrs. Edward Tuckerman. Beyond the railroad bridge is the home of the Misses Snell, sisters of the late Professor E.S. Snell of Amherst College. Ever since the death of Professor Snell, the weather statistics of the College have been kept and published from this house.

A short distance from here, on Snell Street, is the residence of Professor E.P. Harris of Amherst College.

At Mill Valley, a mile from the village, on South Pleasant Street, is a picturesque group of comfortable farmhouses.

Northampton Street is the direct road to Northampton. On the corner opposite College Hall is the Psi Upsilon House, and next to it is the Chi Psi Lodge. Still further from the Common are the Theta Delta Chi House and the homes of Professor Henry Gibbons, Professor H.H. Neill of Amherst College, O.D. Hunt, a prominent merchant, and Professor B.K. Emerson, Professor A.D. Morse, and Dr. C.A. Tuttle of Amherst College.

At the corner of Parsons Street, the first left, is the Zion's Congregational church, established and supported by the students of Amherst College. The building was erected in 1868, and in 1891 Rev. Milton Waldo was the pastor.

On Lincoln Street, near the Theta Delta Chi House, is the home of Rev. G.S. Burroughs, pastor of Amherst College.

Dr. Marshall Henshaw and Dr. H.N. Morse live on Orchard Street. On this street and on Northampton Street are entrances to the athletic field of Amherst College.

North Amherst—The road from Amherst follows along the rich highlands, descending a short hill or two, and rising again as it nears the village. Here everything clusters about a pleasant square, the stately white church, a brick school, stores, and neat dwellings. Just beyond the settlement the historic Mill River, once the northern boundary of the town, flows westward to the Connecticut. North

North Amherst Center.

South Amherst Center.

Amherst "city" is a mile to the east, and Factory Hollow, a diminutive but active manufacturing settlement, is a short distance to the north.

The church building of the North Congregational Society was built in 1826. It contains a fine organ, the gift of Mrs. G.E. Fisher. The society was organized November 15, 1826. Rev. George H. Johnson was the pastor in 1891.

The school building is occupied by a primary and a grammar school. The North Amherst Library Association has a collection of nearly two thousand volumes for public use in this building.

The post-office was established about 1839. The nearest railroad station is at the "City."

Among the residences here are those of Henry W. Haskins, several years one of the selectmen of the town, Edmund Hobart, and Jonathan Cowles, whose farm is one of the largest in the State.

North Amherst "City" is not so large as its name would lead one to believe. The confiding visitor expects something more than the single street, with its railroad station, store, church, and school-house. Beside some cheerful houses, and a factory or two, that is all there is. The village cemetery is a short distance on the road to Amherst.

The Methodist Society, whose little meeting-house stands near the railroad track, was not regularly organized until March 9, 1849, four years after the dedication of the building. Extensive repairs were made upon the house in 1876. The pastor in 1891 was Rev. S.A. Bragg.

There is no post-office at the "City"; all the mail goes to North Amherst, or is opened informally at the railroad station by the postmaster, who drives over for it.

The little Queen Anne school-house was built in 1890. Among the residences is that of A.R. Cushman, whose leather-board mills are some distance beyond the centre of the village.

East Amherst, or "East Street," as it is locally and perhaps better known, is a mile eastward from the main village, Amherst. Like that place, it is built around a grassy remnant of one of the old wide roads, the east street, laid out in 1704. This village in the early part of the century was the active centre of the town. As late as the year 1825, town-meetings were held in the church which then stood at the head of the Common, where the iron water trough now is. The post-office is a branch of that at Amherst.

The Second Congregational church was built in 1889, the first meeting-house of the society having been erected in 1790. Since 1886 Rev. F.J. Fairbanks has been pastor.

The present beautiful Common was laid out by the enterprise of several public-spirited citizens, among them Charles O. Parmenter, at one time representative to the General Court.

East Amherst had the first post-office of the town. It was in the house now occupied by Willard M. Kellogg, on East Street, some distance north of the village store, and was opened about the year 1815, Rufus Kellogg being postmaster. The mails arrived only once a week at those times, and it is within the memory of Mr. Willard Kellogg that his father was summoned from the hayfield by the blowing of a horn to change the mail while the carrier, who came on horseback, sought rest and refreshment. Rufus Kellogg, after a few years, moved the office to the main village, keeping it in the building now occupied by Frank Wood. At the right on the Pelham road, just beyond its corner, near the residence of Noah Dickinson, and the Common, there stood in 1787 a tavern kept by Oliver Clapp, a friend and sympathizer of Daniel Shays, the leader of Shays' Rebellion. Landlord Clapp is said to have given aid and comfort in various ways to the insurgent captain. On the retreat of Shays from Springfield, January 28, 1787, with his eleven hundred men, a halt was made at the hostelry, but not for a long stay, as General Lincoln, commanding the State militia, was following in the rear. Just after Captain Shays had departed toward Pelham, eleven sleigh-loads of his provisions stopped at the tavern, where the horses were about to be fed, but the loyal innkeeper hurried them after the retreating rebels, who were in great need of the stores, and would have been seriously affected if General Lincoln had appeared in time to take the loaded sleighs.

After Clapp's tavern was given up, another was built at the north end of the Common. This is still standing, though it has outlived its first use by many years.

On the east side of the Common is the old residence of General Ebenezer Mattoon, a major in the Revolution, member of Congress in 1801, a sheriff of Hampshire Country, major-general and adjutant-general of the State militia, and captain of the Ancient and Honorable Artillery Company of Boston. He was born in 1755, and died in 1843.

A short distance from the village Common, on the road to Belchertown, are the grounds of the Hampshire County Agricultural Society.[48]

South Amherst is a small farming village in the southeastern part of the town. It has a church, a post-office, and store, and not far away are stations of the Massachusetts Central and New London Northern Railroads.

The South Congregational church was first organized in 1824, and reorganized in 1858. The church building, erected in 1825, was remodelled in 1843. The first pastor was Rev. H.B. Chapin. Rev. H.W. Boyd was pastor in 1891.

The post-office was established in 1838.

The town almshouse, and farm, near the east street, was rebuilt, after a destructive fire, in 1882. It is valued at about $8,000, and yields the town, under the superintendence of Henry C. Dickinson, a good return upon its value.

Chapter 5

# Amherst College

Amherst College was opened September 18, 1821, under the name of the "Collegiate Charitable Institution." On this day the first president was inaugurated, and the first building dedicated.

As long before as 1762, the people of Hampshire County had made several ineffectual attempts to obtain a charter from the General Court and the Governor of the Province of Massachusetts to incorporate a "seminary of learning." The matter seems to have been forgotten in the excitement of the approaching war; but the interest then awakened was only in abeyance, and afterward resulted in the founding of Williams College and the establishment of Amherst Academy. It was from this latter institution that the Amherst College developed.

The Academy was opened in 1814. The residents of Hampshire and the surrounding counties subscribed the money needed for its support, and in 1816 the State granted it a charter. The building stood upon the site of the present grammar school-house on Amity Street; and the land was the gift of Dr. David Parsons, afterward made president of the Board of Trustees. Many distinguished names are to be found upon the books of the Academy, connected with it as teachers and pupils. For years it ranked among the first schools of Massachusetts.

In 1818, when the trustees were engaged in collecting a scholarship fund of $10,000 for "indigent young men with the ministry in view," it became evident that the people were willing to give a larger sum for an institution of a higher grade. Accordingly, after more than $51,000 had been gathered in conditional subscriptions, it was voted to found the "Collegiate Charitable Institution." The money thus obtained was the first that Amherst College had, and to-day it is entered on the books of the treasurer as the "Charitable Fund."

The laying of the corner-stone of the first building of the Charitable Institution, the present South College, is thus mentioned in the reports of the occasion: "On the ninth of August instant (1820) the Board of Trustees of Amherst Academy, together with the subscribers to the fund then present, a number of the neighboring clergy, and the preceptors and students of the Academy, preceded by the building committee and the workmen, moved in procession from the Academy to the ground of the Charity Institution." The dedication exercises, the fall of the year following, were simple, and opened with an address by Noah Webster, president of the Board of Trustees. The institution began September 19, with forty-seven students and three instructors.

After the young college had been fairly launched upon its career, the trustees, who were still trustees of the Academy, turned their attention toward obtaining a State charter, which should give them the privileges of a recognized college. It was a long struggle against well-organized opposition from Harvard, Brown, and Williams colleges. State politics were affected not a little by it, but the publicity of the agitation only brought popularity to the infant institution. When the charter, which changed the name to Amherst College, was finally granted, February 25, 1825, the number of the students and instructors had increased nearly threefold. Upon those students who had graduated prior to the granting of the charter the trustees immediately conferred the honorary degrees due to them.

The first president of Amherst College was the Rev. Zephaniah Swift Moore, D.D. He had been president of Williams College, resigning that office to accept the position at Amherst. His official term was from September, 1821, to June 29, 1823 when he died. The following list gives the names and terms of office of the succeeding presidents of the College: Heman Humphrey, D.D (1823-1845); Edward Hitchcock, D.D., LL.D (1845-1854); William Augustus Stearns, D.D., LL.D (1854-1876); Julius Hawley Seelye, D.D., LL.D (1876-1890).

Merrill Edwards Gates, Ph.D., LL.D., L.H.D., chosen president July 30, 1890, assumed the duties of the office October 27 of the same year. His formal inauguration occurred at the following commencement.

View from the Amherst College Library.

View from the Amherst College Chapel.

The government of the College is vested in a Board of Trustees, whose corporate name is "The Trustees of Amherst College." Its membership can never be more than seventeen, of whom seven must be clergymen and the remainder laymen.

The College is not sectarian, and there are no sectarian or denominational restrictions as to the membership of the Board.

Five positions are now filled by the alumni of the College, though for nearly fifty years the legislature of the State exercised this power. The Board holds two regular meetings, usually one during commencement week, and the other in the fall of each year, special meetings being called by the president when necessary. The control of the internal affairs of the College is in the hands of the faculty, of whom the president is the executive officer. This body in 1891 comprised twenty-two professors and nine lecturers and instructors.

In 1882, at the suggestion of President Seelye, the faculty associated with them in the direction of college affairs a body of ten students, known as the College Senate. The members are elected by their classes, acting under established regulations,—four seniors, three juniors, two sophomores, and one freshman. The president of the College presides at the meetings of the Senate and may veto any of its actions. All questions of decorum and discipline may be brought before it, and offenders may be punished by suspension or expulsion from college.

Since its beginning the plan has proved successful in lessening the number of restriction rules of the College, bringing the students and teachers in close yet dignified relations, and developing a manlier spirit among the students. In a letter to the alumni of the College in the fall of 1888 President Seelye said:

*The action of the faculty in referring to the decision of the Senate all questions of college order and decorum has been justified by the result. The Senate have considered such questions, from the first, intelligently and without passion; and during the past year there has been an evident growth in their sense of responsibility, and in the weight given to their judgments by the College. The decisions of the Senate have sometimes gone entirely counter to the prevailing wishes of the students; but they have been accepted, so far as I know, without dissent. The Senate seems now able, not merely to voice, but to direct, college sentiment on matters submitted to their jurisdiction; and I cannot but think that there is in this an educating force of great worth and promise.*

The Amherst method of student government has recently been copied by several prominent institutions. The Senate meets monthly at the president's office.

The departments of instruction may be divided into Philosophy, History and Art, Language and Literature, and Science. The student is offered his choice of a classical or a scientific course, the former entitling him at graduation to the degree of Bachelor of Arts, and the latter to that of Bachelor of Science.

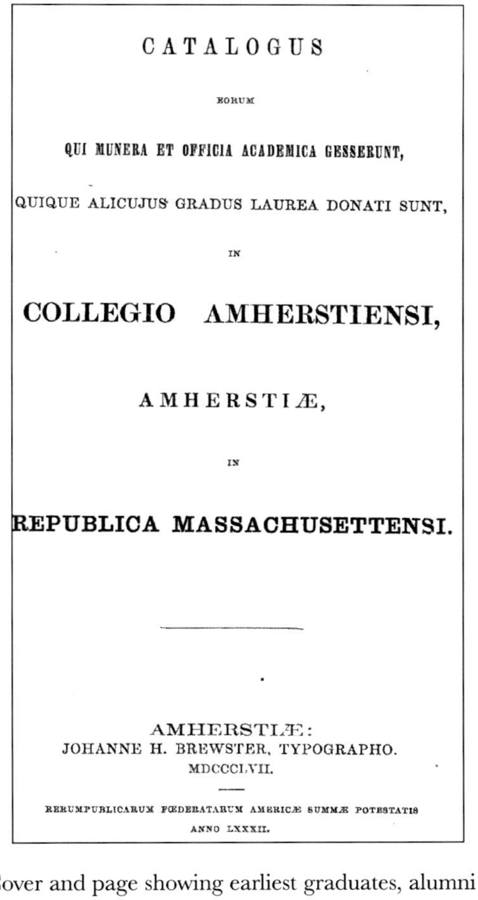

CATALOGUS

EORUM

QUI MUNERA ET OFFICIA ACADEMICA GESSERUNT,

QUIQUE ALICUJUS GRADUS LAUREA DONATI SUNT,

IN

COLLEGIO AMHERSTIENSI,

AMHERSTIÆ,

IN

REPUBLICA MASSACHUSETTENSI.

AMHERSTIÆ:
JOHANNE H. BREWSTER, TYPOGRAPHO.
MDCCCLVII.

RERUMPUBLICARUM FŒDERATARUM AMERICÆ SUMMÆ POTESTATIS
ANNO LXXXII.

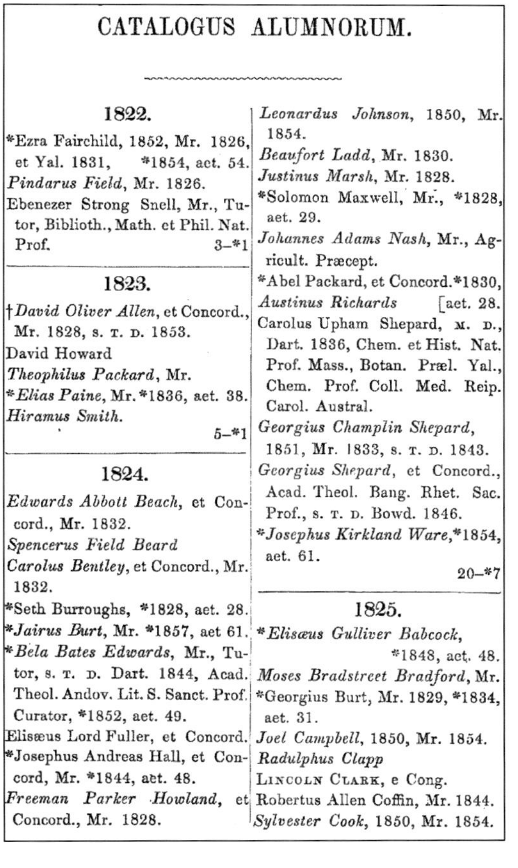

CATALOGUS ALUMNORUM.

1822.

*Ezra Fairchild, 1852, Mr. 1826, et Yal. 1831, *1854, aet. 54.
*Pindarus Field*, Mr. 1826.
Ebenezer Strong Snell, Mr., Tutor, Biblioth., Math. et Phil. Nat. Prof. 3–*1

1823.

†*David Oliver Allen*, et Concord., Mr. 1828, S. T. D. 1853.
David Howard
*Theophilus Packard*, Mr.
**Elias Paine*, Mr. *1836, aet. 38.
*Hiramus Smith*. 5–*1

1824.

*Edwards Abbott Beach*, et Concord., Mr. 1832.
*Spencerus Field Beard*
*Carolus Bentley*, et Concord., Mr. 1832.
*Seth Burroughs, *1828, aet. 28.
**Jairus Burt*, Mr. *1857, aet 61.
**Bela Bates Edwards*, Mr., Tutor, S. T. D. Dart. 1844, Acad. Theol. Andov. Lit. S. Sanct. Prof. Curator, *1852, aet. 49.
Elisæus Lord Fuller, et Concord.
*Josephus Andreas Hall, et Concord, Mr. *1844, aet. 48.
*Freeman Parker Howland*, et Concord., Mr. 1828.
*Leonardus Johnson*, 1850, Mr. 1854.
*Beaufort Ladd*, Mr. 1830.
*Justinus Marsh*, Mr. 1828.
*Solomon Maxwell, Mr., *1828, aet. 29.
*Johannes Adams Nash*, Mr., Agricult. Præcept.
*Abel Packard, et Concord. *1830, [aet. 28.
*Austinus Richards*
Carolus Upham Shepard, M. D., Dart. 1836, Chem. et Hist. Nat. Prof. Mass., Botan. Præl. Yal., Chem. Prof. Coll. Med. Reip. Carol. Austral.
*Georgius Champlin Shepard*, 1851, Mr. 1833, S. T. D. 1843.
*Georgius Shepard*, et Concord., Acad. Theol. Bang. Rhet. Sac. Prof., S. T. D. Bowd. 1846.
**Josephus Kirkland Ware*, *1854, aet. 61. 20–*7

1825.

**Elisæus Gulliver Babcock*, *1848, aet. 48.
*Moses Bradstreet Bradford*, Mr.
*Georgius Burt, Mr. 1829, *1834, aet. 31.
*Joel Campbell*, 1850, Mr. 1854.
*Radulphus Clapp*
LINCOLN CLARK, e Cong.
Robertus Allen Coffin, Mr. 1844.
*Sylvester Cook*, 1850, Mr. 1854.

Cover and page showing earliest graduates, alumni catalog of Amherst College, 1857. *Image courtesy of editor's collection.*

The work of the first year at Amherst College is prescribed for all students. After the first term of the sophomore year, there is great freedom of choice among an exceedingly broad system of electives. Out of the fourteen to sixteen hours of work in a week for each student through sophomore year, an average of less than five; through junior year, a little more than one; and through senior year, a little more than three,—which includes philosophy and oratory,—are prescribed for each term.

The elective studies, open for choice, include the fullest work in Greek, Latin, French, German, Italian, and Sanskrit; ample courses in rhetoric and oratory, logic, English literature, biology, both cryptogamic and phenogramic; zoology, physiology, and general biology, and full opportunity for laboratory work in chemistry. In geology and mineralogy the College has held a leading place ever since the work of President Hitchcock made its name as well known in England and Germany as in America. For physics, the new laboratory will afford, in addition to the general work, ample facilities for full courses in electricity and its application. There are full courses in practical and theoretical astronomy with observatory work; and thorough instruction in history, political economy, political ethics, and the duties of citizenship; in psychology, moral philosophy, metaphysics, and the history of philosophy, and biblical literature. Physical culture is prescribed throughout the college course.

Attendance upon college exercises is required. An allowance for necessary absences is made by permitting the student to remain away from one-tenth of the total number of exercises of each course in a term, without requiring an equivalent. An excess of this proportion of absences is made up by specially assigned work, the amount of which is determined by the degree of the delinquency. In the case of excess of absences from Sunday services and morning prayers, special work in some of the regular courses is required.[49]

The number of students in the College has averaged 344 during the ten years ending 1891. It is a matter of some interest to note that during the last few years about one-seventh of all the entering students have come to Amherst from other institutions.[50] In 1891 the students represented thirty States of the Union. The following table gives the number of students and teachers, at intervals of five years, since the founding of the College. It indicates the fact that the largest number in college, until after the year 1866, was 259 in 1836, and that between these years there was a period of great depression. Since 1851 the increase has been gradual, but almost constant.

| | | |
|---|---|---|
| 1821: 59 | 1846: 120 | 1871: 261 |
| 1826: 170 | 1851: 190 | 1876: 338 |
| 1831: 195 | 1856: 229[51] | 1881: 339 |
| 1836: 259 | 1861: 235 | 1886: 331 |
| 1841: 142 | 1866: 203 | 1891: 351 |

Amherst College receives students from a large number of preparatory schools, some of the best of which are allowed to enter their pupils on certificate of the work done.

*Above*: A drawing of College Hall, 1891.

*Below*: College Hall, early twentieth century. *Image courtesy of editor's collection.*

The following are some of the leading ones: Adelphi Academy, Brooklyn, N.Y.; Boston Latin School, Boston, Mass.; Chicago High School, Chicago, Ill.; Newton High School, Newton, Mass.; Phillips Academy, Andover, Mass.; Phillips Academy, Exeter, N.H.; Polytechnic Institute, Brooklyn, N.Y.; Roxbury Latin School, Roxbury, Mass.; Saxton River Academy, Saxton River; Springfield High School, Springfield, Mass.; St. Johnsbury Academy, St. Johnsbury, Vt.; Williston Seminary, Easthampton, Mass.; Worcester Academy, Worcester, Mass.; Worcester High School, Worcester, Mass.

The amount of pecuniary assistance that Amherst is able to give its worthy students is constantly increasing.

An enthusiastic scholar of slender means need not leave the College for want of aid.[52] Opportunities for earning money are frequently offered by the residents of the town, and desirable positions where a student can aid himself by rendering service in the different departments of the College are reserved exclusively for those who require financial assistance in obtaining their education. In addition to this, the beneficiary funds are divided liberally and justly. The amounts available are shown in this table:

| | |
|---|---|
| Charitable fund | $83,000 |
| Scholarship fund | $70,400 |
| Private scholarship gifts | $470 |
| Fellowships | $550 |
| Prizes | $1,779 |
| Total | $156,196 |

The cost of an education at Amherst is so often a matter of serious concern within the family circle that reliable data cannot fail to be appreciated. Published estimates are often found to differ from experience. Careful inquiries have been made among trustworthy students of the College, and the estimates given below are based upon actual experiences. The effort has been to err, if at all, in overstating rather than understating those expenses which vary with a student's personal habits. The smallest annual expenditure reported was $308.50, which included every item of cost except the long vacation. A large number of students spend less than $400, and this can be done without suffering of any kind. The majority of students are believed to spend between $475 and $675 each year. In the following table the annual expenditures are itemized upon four different scales. The actual cost of each item has been carefully obtained and entered, without taking into consideration the fact that it is almost universally the custom in college to reduce the net expenses by renting furniture, or buying it, as well as books, at second hand, and of disposing of them at the close of the course or of the year. These and other very useful methods of economizing may well be considered by students who wish to estimate in advance the expense of going through college. The upper limit of expenditure is of course indeterminable. The estimate in this case is made on the assumption that the student rooms alone, while in the three lower tables, the expenses of room-rent, fuel, lights, and furniture are entered as if shared with a room-mate.

The Department of Physical Education and Hygiene deserves especial attention here, because it was the first to be established as a part of the regular course in any American college. In fact, the systems of physical culture now in use in nearly

| | Least. | Economical. | Liberal. | Expensive. |
|---|---|---|---|---|
| Tuition . . . . . . | $110.00 | $110.00 | $110.00 | $110.00 |
| Books . . . . . . | 8.00 | 15.00 | 20.00 | 35.00 |
| Room . . . . . . | (b) 12.00 | 30.00 | 75.00 | 200.00 |
| Fuel and Lights . . . | 11.00 | 15.00 | 25.00 | 40.00 |
| Board . . . . . . | 111.00 | 129.50 | 148.00 | 222.00 |
| Furniture (annual average) . . . . . . | 10.00 | 15.00 | 30.00 | 40.00 |
| Clothing . . . . . | 50.00 | 70.00 | 150.00 | 200.00 |
| Washing . . . . . | 10.00 | 15.00 | 25.00 | 40.00 |
| Society Fees . . . . | — | (a) 20.00 | (a) 20.00 | (a) 20.00 |
| Stationery . . . . . | 5.00 | 10.00 | 15.00 | 20.00 |
| Subscriptions . . . . | — | 5.00 | 20.00 | 40.00 |
| Sundries . . . . . | 30.00 | 35.00 | 50.00 | 60.00 |
| Totals . . . . . | $357.00 | $469.50 | $688.00 | $1,027.00 |

(*a*) This sum is believed to be a fair average. (*b*) In the dormitory.

all the institutions of learning in this country are largely copies, or embody many features, of the Amherst system. To the late President Stearns belongs the credit of suggesting that daily exercise under the supervision of a physician should be a required portion of the college student's life. He had found that, if left to themselves, the students neglected to care for their health, and frequently graduated from college physically wrecked. The plan he proposed was at length adopted by the trustees, and a regular professorship founded. In 1860 the Barrett Gymnasium was built for the department, and the year following Dr. Edward Hitchcock, the son of President Hitchcock, and the present incumbent of the position, was appointed. The history of the department is the history of the life of its chief. He developed a system at first unknown, then distrusted, but now approved by the most eminent educators.

The present organization of the department brings within its scope everything which has a bearing upon the physical welfare of the college students. Its purposes may be conveniently classed under these five heads:

Personal acquaintance with the physical condition of every student.

Requirement of the amount of daily exercise which experience has shown to be most beneficial, and the direction of all who take special exercise.

Examination of every student at intervals during the college course, and preservation of all statistics thus taken.

Class instruction in anatomy, physiology, and hygiene.

Control of the general athletics of the College.

These functions are fully performed. At all times during the college year Dr. Hitchcock is thoroughly conversant with the general health of every student. Overwork is scarcely possible under such care, and when sickness does occur, the case is carefully followed by the department, which interferes, however, in no way with the physician in charge. Students may at any time consult Dr. Hitchcock.

Regular exercise in the Gymnasium is required of every student in college. Each class assembles four days in the week for a half-hour's pleasant drill with wooden dumb-bells. There are always class officers to lead the exercise under the direction of the professor or his assistants. In a modified way, well adapted to the purposes of the department, the organization of the classes is like that of a military body. An annual prize drill occurs in May, the three upper classes competing. The prize on this occasion is $100, given by Dr. Rufus P. Lincoln, of the class of 1862, to the class obtaining the highest mark in the dumb-bell drill and marching. Athletically inclined students, particularly those in training for any of the college teams, are given every needed suggestion and direction.

Perhaps the most interesting portion of the work of Dr. Hitchcock, and certainly the most valuable to the department, is the system of anthropometry, or recording of physical statistics. Three times during the college course the student is examined, measured, and tested in every essential function of the body. If found defective or undeveloped in any parts, he is advised what he may do to reach, or exceed, the usual standard. From the immense number of measurements made in the past thirty years, the department is able to give a valuable and interesting average of measurements as a basis for advice and the future exercise of the student. The examination that is thus made is more minute than that required in the United States army. An important feature of the system, as practised at Amherst, is the publication of the averages for the use of all who may be benefited by them.

Dr. Hitchcock conducts classes in the subjects that are important as giving the young man a thorough knowledge of the proper care of his health. This study is required early in the college course.

In the direction of the general athletics of the College, the department exercises only a reasonable supervision of the members of the base-ball, foot-ball, and athletic teams of the College. The control in the matter of conducting the contests for championships with other colleges, and the financial management of the teams, is lodged in the Athletic Board, organized in 1891, and consisting of three members of the college faculty, four alumni of the College, who are not members of the faculty, and the managers of the three teams. Of these members, Dr. Hitchcock, as the head of the department, and F.B. Pratt of the class of 1887, as the donor of the Pratt Field, are life members.

Dr. Hitchcock has as an assistant, a practising physician in the town, and since 1890 there has been a second assistant under the provisions of the Lincoln fellowship fund.

The President's House.

The President's House, College Library and College Hall (left to right), early twentieth century. *Image courtesy of editor's collection.*

## The Summer School of Languages

During a portion of the long vacation of Amherst College, the Summer School of Languages, under the direction of Professor W.L. Montague, is in session. The school was established in 1877 by Dr. L. Sauveur of New York City. From the beginning, Professor Montague has been actively connected with its management, assuming the entire control in 1883, when Dr. Sauveur retired. The school term opens shortly after the College has closed, and continues five weeks—a period which is always pleasantly and profitably occupied with recitations,—frequently in the open air,—lectures, excursions, and many social affairs.

The College Chapel forms the headquarters of the Summer School. In this building are the director's office and the rooms of most of the recitations. Walker Hall opens several of its rooms for recitations; Williston Hall for work in chemistry; and the privileges of the Gymnasium, Appleton Cabinet, the Observatory, and the Library are all offered to the members of the school.

Making no pretensions at the first to be anything more than a school of languages, the courses of study have been gradually broadened until, in 1891, they were embraced in twelve distinct courses, as follows: French, German, Greek and Latin, Italian, Spanish, English Literature, Art, Chemistry, Anglo-Saxon and Early English, Physical Education, Library Economy, and Mathematics. All of these courses are graded so that the best advantages are offered to persons of every degree of accomplishment. A most enjoyable feature of the French and German departments has always been the boarding-tables, at which native teachers preside and all English words are strictly discountenanced. The amount of study is entirely optional. Frequent lectures upon interesting subjects are delivered each week.

The board of teachers of the school comprised eighteen members in 1891, and three special lecturers. Professor Montague is himself a thorough language student, being at the head of the departments of French, Italian, and Spanish in Amherst College. The instructors in French, German, and Italian are natives of foreign countries, all highly educated, and speaking their language in its purity and perfection.

The members of the school are, to a great extent, teachers of various schools throughout the country, coming to Amherst to increase their knowledge and improve the methods which can be gained only from native instructors. Besides these, there are always many people who study for their own pleasure, and young men and women in preparation for college or special work. The average attendance in the five years ending in 1890 has been over two hundred, and nearly every State and Territory in the Union has been represented.

An especial aim of the school is to furnish the best instruction and to reduce the expenses of those attending to a minimum. The accompanying table gives the necessary items of expenditure:

All the languages and lectures, excepting Anglo-Saxon and Early English, $16
Anglo-Saxon and Early English, $8
Chemistry, full day, $22
Chemistry, half day, $12

Art, out-door sketching, $8
Art, in-door work, $12
Art, normal work, $8
Art, wood-carving, $8
Physical training, full course $10
Physical training, half course $5
Mathematics, one subject $10
Mathematics, two subjects $15
Library Economy $10

To members of the School of Languages a reduction of $2 from each item under Chemistry, Art, Physical Training, and Mathematics is allowed. If only lectures are attended, the charge is $1 each course.

The sessions of the school have always proved successful from a social as well as a scholarly standpoint. Amherst offers a wealth of natural enjoyment that is never unappreciated, and excursions, drives, and picnics are as numerous as there are days in the school. Taken all in all, the life of a summer school student is far from being irksome.

## The College Buildings

One of the chief features of a visit to Amherst is a walk through the college grounds, with a glance at the buildings and their interesting histories. With the exception of College Hall, the Church, and the Cabinets, all will be found open during the greater part of the day when the College or the Summer School of Languages is in session. The Cabinets may be seen during fixed hours each week-day, usually from ten o'clock to five, between May 15th and November 1st, and from ten to twelve and three to four at other seasons; or they will be opened at any time on application to the custodians, whose residences are usually bulletined at the entrances.

Perhaps the most convenient starting-point for such a tour is at the corner of Northampton Street and the Common, where stands

College Hall, which was built in 1830, by the First Congregational Society of Amherst, and used by them as a place of worship until 1867, when purchased by the College for $8,000.[53] The building is now used for the public lectures, commencement, and other exercises of the College, and has a seating capacity of eight hundred, which may be increased by nearly two hundred if the platform be brought into service. Next to College Hall is the

Henry T. Morgan Library, enlarged to its present size in 1882. The original building included the square portion at the northeast corner and the tower, and was built in 1853 at an expense of $10,000. This was the first stone building of the College. The new portion, comprising the librarian's office and the rooms above it at the side, and the large book room at the rear, was designed by Allen & Kenway of Boston, and was completed at a cost of $48,381, which included the entire renovation of the original building. The whole structure is of Pelham granite. In the hallway, at the right of the entrance, and in the old portion, is a room for small gatherings and recitations, used as headquarters of the alumni at commencement; beyond it is a packingroom, both of these opening into a large cataloguing-room. The librarian's office is at the end of the hallway. On the walls at the right of this hall are valuable specimens of Assyrian art, in the shape of eight huge sculptured stone slabs, bearing colossal mythological figures in relief and hieroglyphic inscriptions. Their actual cost was about $600; their value many thousands. These slabs were presented to the College in 1855 by the late Rev. Henry Lobdell, of the class of 1849, a missionary to Assyria, who died at Mosul in 1850. They were taken from the palace of Sardanapalus, the last king of Assyria, and their inscriptions belong to a period nine hundred years before Christ. In 1871 Rev. W.H. Ward, D.D., of the class of 1856, and since 1870 editor of the *New York Independent*, greatly enhanced the value of these works of ancient art by translating, from the cuneiform characters, into English the inscriptions, which were found to be a record of a conquest. The manuscript translations are preserved in a bound volume in the Library, and are very interesting even to those not professing to be archaeological students. At the head of the stairs is the book-delivery room of the Library, opening from which is the reading-room, which occupies the entire second story of the original building, and formerly contained all the books of the Library.

The reference books and periodical literature are kept here. This is a large, finely decorated room, lighted by long windows, and a lantern in the roof. In the side opposite the entrance are beautiful stained glass windows of appropriate design. They are the gift of Hon. Frederic Ayer of Lowell. Beginning at the left of the entrance of the room, the paintings on the walls are in this order: the first five presidents of the College, Drs. Moore, Humphrey, Hitchcock, Stearns, and Seelye; Professor W.S. Tyler, Professor N.W. Fiske, Professor C.B. Adams, Professor C.U. Shepard, Professor Aaron Warner, who were all at the same time members of the faculty; and Joel Giles of Townsend, Hon. David Sears of Boston, Hon. Samuel Williston of Easthampton, Hon. Chester W. Chapin of Springfield, S.H. Winkley of Philadelphia, Hon. G.H. Gilbert of Ware, Rev. Dr. Brace of Hartford, Conn., who have been liberal benefactors of the College. The portraits in the book-delivery room are of President Stearns and Hon. David Sears. The attendants will readily grant permission to inspect the book room, and visitors will find it very interesting. There are six floors for the storage of the books, each 50 by 41 feet in area and 7½ in height. They are entirely of iron latticework, which, with the walls of solid masonry and iron door, renders the entire room as nearly fireproof as it is possible it could be. The shelves are capable of holding 20,000 volumes on each floor, or more than 120,000 in all. At the first of January, 1891, there were 55,000 volumes in the Library, and the annual increase is between 2,000 and 2,500. In 1867, the libraries of the Athena and the Alexandrian societies, then in very active existence, were merged into the college Library, and for some years the members of these organizations paid an annual fee to the College for the care and increase of the volumes. The students have always been allowed almost complete freedom of access to the book room and its contents. The building bears the name of Henry T. Morgan of Albany, whose

The Henry T. Morgan Library, 1891.

The Henry T. Morgan Library, 1908. The trees in front are bigger and ivy now grows on the façade of the building. *Image courtesy of editor's collection.*

generous gifts to the College aided in erecting the new portion of the Library. In 1891, William I. Fletcher was the librarian.

Next to the Library stands the

President's House. This was erected by the trustees of the College in the year 1834, and cost $9,000. The first house erected for the president of the College is still standing, and, in a remodelled condition, is the chapter house of the Psi Upsilon Fraternity. President Humphrey occupied the present house immediately after its erection. For a number of years previous to 1891 it was a private school for young ladies, and after being again remodelled became the home of President M.E. Gates.[54]

Crossing the head of the Common, in front of the Library, the

College Fence is noticed at the right. This is an institution peculiar to college men. It is usually the scene of the celebration of the victories of the College, and almost any summer evening a group of students can be found gathered upon it, making the air melodious with college songs. It was presented by the class of 1889 and dedicated by appropriate exercises, in which the faculty and students took part, in the spring of 1887. Custom prohibits the freshman class, unless having won some honor for the College, from using this fence.

Passing into the college grounds, the brick building at the right is

Williston Hall, which occupies the site of the former North College dormitory. The dormitory was built in 1827 at an expense of $10,000, and was burned early in the spring of 1857. The loss occurred during the darkest days of Amherst's history, but it proved an unexpected benefit. Scarcely had the flames been extinguished when the late Hon. Samuel Williston of Easthampton announced that he would erect a new building, containing recitation rooms and laboratories that had long been needed by the College. Williston Hall was thus dedicated May 19, 1858, and cost $15,000. The main entrance of the building is on the north side, and in the hallway is an interesting memorial of the Amherst College students who fought in the Rebellion. It is a six-pound brass cannon, which was captured at Newbern, N.C., March 14, 1862, and upon it is engraved its history and the names of the Amherst students—four officers and sixteen privates—who were killed in the battle. After its capture, the cannon was presented by General Bunrnside to the Twenty-first Regiment, M.V., who in turn gave it to the trustees of Amherst College "as an enduring monument to the memory of their lamented brothers who fell while fighting for liberty and union."

The Mather Collection of Art occupies the entire upper story of the building. It is probably the finest collection of plaster casts in the United States, excepting only that at Boston, Mass. The honor of the suggestion, as well as of the actual gathering of money and purchasing of the collection belongs to the memory of the late Professor Richard H. Mather. Professor Mather solicited, largely from personal friends, the first $10,000 of the fund, and made the selections himself when visiting Europe. The casts began to arrive in 1874, and during Professor Mather's life not a year passed without the addition of something desirable. The collection has long since outgrown its present room, and until better accommodations are provided few additions can be made, although a fund is constantly accumulating.[55]

Williston Hall.

The Mather Art Collection.

As an example of the care that Professor Mather took in making the collection, it may be remarked that it contains the only cast in existence of the bronze doors of the Senate Chamber at Washington.

The design for these doors was modelled by Crawford, and they were cast at Chicopee, Mass. At the opposite end of the gallery are casts of the Ghiberti doors at Florence, Italy. The frescoing about the room is pure Greek in style.

The Greek lecture room on the second story is reached from the art gallery by the smaller stairway. This was originally the hall of the Athence Society. The corresponding room on the same floor—reached from the door at the eastern side of the tower—was at the same time occupied by the Alexandrian Society. This latter room is used, pending the completion of the new chemical laboratory, as the laboratory for advanced work. The chemistry lecture room is at the left of the south entrance on the ground floor, and the general laboratory is at the right. Crossing the driveway in front of Williston Hall, the stone building at the left is

Walker Hall—This building was completed as it now stands in 1883, and cost $87,250.[56] Twelve years previously, a building of the same general design was erected on the same site through the generosity of Dr. W.J. Walker of Charlestown, Mass. The original Walker Hall was burned March, 1882, and with it was destroyed one of the most valuable collections of minerals in the country. A portion of the outside wall of the building alone remained, and after it had been strengthened on the inside, became a part of the new Walker Hall. The expense of the rebuilding was met by the late Henry T. Morgan of Albany, N.Y., and in return he was honored by having his name attached to the College Library. The rooms of the building are assigned as follows: 1, registrar's office; 2, treasurer's office; 4, physics workroom; 5, pastor's office; 3 and 6, recitation rooms; 7 and 8,

Walker Hall.

The Barrett Gymnasium.

physics lecture room and laboratory; 9, president's office; 10, recitation room; 11, astronomical lecture room; 12, 13, and 14, recitation rooms.

The rooms of the physics department are open for inspection. The laboratory contains about $9,000 worth of apparatus, of which $2,000 worth was constructed especially for the College in Paris. The lecture room has upon the wall, at the right of the entrance, a brass tablet to the memory of the late Professor Elihu Root, placed there by the class of 1881.

The Barrett Gymnasium, erected in 1860 at a cost of $10,000, was largely the means of developing the system of physical culture for which Amherst is justly famous. It was the first building in the country erected for gymnastic work in charge of a regularly appointed professor. It is of Pelham granite, and is 70 feet long by 50 wide. It was designed by C.E. Parkes of Boston, and bears the name of Dr. Benjamin Barrett of Northampton, who was a large contributor toward the fund for its erection and support. Since the completion of the Pratt Gymnasium in 1884, the building has been used for various purposes, while awaiting alterations to make it a geological cabinet.

When used as a gymnasium, the physician's office, dressing-rooms, and bowling-alleys were on the ground floor, with the main hall for class and special exercise above.

The College Church, designed by W.A. Potter of New York, was erected in 1870–71, and cost $70,000, of which the late William F. Stearns, son of President Stearns, contributed $47,000. The site for the building was chosen for its remarkable beauty. A dormitory known as "East College" stood between it and the tree-sheltered path leading to the college well. This dormitory was taken down shortly after the church was completed. The view from the rear of the church is one of the finest within the limits of Amherst. Two miles across the valley, the Pelham hills rise in gentle outline, the range extending from the north, as far as can be seen, until near the southern limit of the town it is lost in the Belchertown hills. The valley, broad and fertile, is well populated in parts, and contains nearly all the manufactories

The College Church.

of the town. Toward the south it spreads out into generous farmlands through which run two thread-like railways. The grandeur of this landscape when the foliage has become brilliant in the fall, is unsurpassed by any in the western part of the Commonwealth. This crest of the College Hill is visited by lovers of nature in every season of the year.

The church building itself is not out of harmony with its surroundings. Its gray sides and brown sandstone trimmings are plentifully covered with the soft, clinging ivies planted by the college classes at their graduation. At the entrances and between the windows are soft-hued shafts of marble. Curious carvings decorate the brown stones in the gable ends of the building. "Dei Glorize" and "A.D. 1870" are on the north side; the cross and other symbols of the Christian Church, with small reliefs of the four evangelists, between the windows, on the east side; a lantern, thorn branch, passion flower, wheat, and grape vine, all typical of incidents in the life of Christ, on the south side; and "Agnus Dei" and "Rex," "Lex," "Dux," "Lux," on the west side. The spire of the church is about one hundred and fifty feet high, and twenty-four feet square at the base. Its four sections are alternately square and octagonal. Within it hangs a chime of eight bells, given by George Howe of Boston, as a memorial of the Amherst boys who fell in the War of the Rebellion. The gift acquires special significance from the fact that the son of Mr. Howe was among the number whose lives were sacrificed for their country. The seats in the main portion of the church are reserved for the families of the faculty, the juniors, and seniors. In the right transept are seated the freshmen, in the left the sophomores. The capacity of the house is about six hundred. The stained glass window in the right transept was given by the Congregational church at Bedford, Mass., President Stearns' native place; that opposite, by Ex-Governor Onslow Stearns of Concord, N.H.; and that in the rear of the church, by the late Eckley Stearns of Woburn, Mass. President Stearns' former church at Cambridgeport, Mass., presented the pulpit. Tablets placed upon the church walls commemorate the useful lives of President Stearns, William F. Stearns, and Professor Richard H. Mather. The corner-stone of the building was laid in the autumn of 1875, and the dedication occurred July 1, 1873.

At the side of the college grounds, and south of the church is

The PRATT GYMNASIUM, begun in the summer of 1883, and completed the following spring at a cost of $68,000. It ranks third among the college gymnasiums of the country, those of Yale and Harvard only being superior in size and cost. The building is of brick with brownstone trimmings, and is 122 feet long and 88 wide. It bears the name of Pratt Gymnasium in recognition of the generosity of Mr. Charles M. Pratt of New York, a graduate of the class of 1879. In the hall, at the right of the main entrance of the building, is a brass tablet, bearing this inscription:

*ERECTED BY*
*CHARLES MILLARD PRATT, OF BROOKLYN, N.Y.,*
*CLASS CAPTAIN OF THE CLASS OF '79,*
*TO INCREASE THE USEFULNESS OF HIS ALMA MATER IN*
*THAT DEPARTMENT IN WHICH HE EVER FELT AN*
*INTEREST, AND TO EXPRESS THE WARM AFFECTION WHICH*
*HE CHERISHED FOR ITS FAITHFUL HEAD,*
*DR. EDWARD HITCHCOCK.*

The office of the professor of hygiene and physical culture and the room for making physical examinations and recording statistics occupy the corner of the first floor, between the main and side entrances. The other rooms on this floor are the large dressing-room, containing 274 heated and ventilated lockers, and

The Pratt Gymnasium.

shower-bath, dry-rub, and small dressing-rooms. The main hall is 80 feet long by 64 wide, and contains such apparatus as is needed for class and individual exercise. It is two stories high, and lighted and ventilated from the sides and roof. A running-gallery, 207 feet 10¾ inches long and 6 feet wide, encircles the hall 11 feet above the floor. In the second story is the "Resort," the headquarters of the college weekly, *The Amherst Student,* and a storeplace for many highly prized trophies and relics of college interest; a billiard room, the only one in the country connected with a college gymnasium, and containing a pool and two billiard tables; and the rooms for the custodians of the building. The basement has a base-ball cage, 76 by 21 feet, three bowling-alleys, 70 feet long, and a sparring-room. Tub and sponge baths of the best patterns, dressing, and furnace rooms occupy the remainder of the basement.

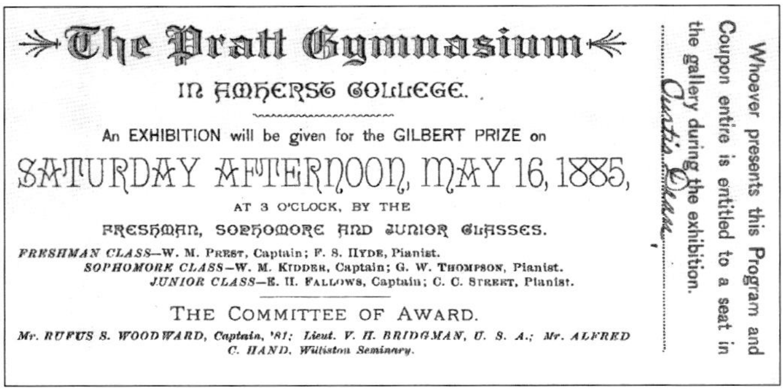


A ticket to a gymnastics exhibition at the Pratt Gymnasium, 1885.
*Image courtesy of editor's collection.*

As the visitor passes up the walk from the main entrance of the Gymnasium, directly in front, is

Appleton Cabinet, erected in 1855, at an expense of $10,000, appropriated for the purpose by the trustees of the will of the late Samuel Appleton of Boston. Mr. Appleton left the sum of $200,000 at the disposal of his executors to be used for benevolent and scientific purposes, and it was in response to the urgent appeals of President Hitchcock, then in office, that the money for this building was obtained. The portion of the Cabinet first approached as the visitor proceeds from the Gymnasium, is the biological laboratory and lecture room, where specimens for class work and illustration are kept.[57]

The main part of the building has been made almost completely fireproof for the protection of the collections that are stored in it. The entrance from the biological lecture room is closed by heavy iron doors. The second story is devoted to the Adams Zoological Museum, a large part of which was the gift of the late Professor C.B. Adams. The collection of insects and shells are kept in the horizontal cases. The latter collection comprises about eight thousand species, and of it Professor Louis Agassiz once said, "I do not know in all the country a conchological collection of equal value." In the gallery at the head of the hall has been placed the Audubon collection of birds, presented to the College in 1886 by the Hon. E.E. Farnam, of the class of 1855. It is valued at $1,200. The cast of the skeleton of the American Megatherium, near the entrance, was the gift of the late Joshua Bates of London, England. The original skeleton was found in Buenos Ayres, South America.

Appleton Cabinet.

The ground-floor of the Cabinet is chiefly occupied by the Hitchcock Ichnological collection, made by the late President Hitchcock between the years 1835 and 1864. President Hitchcock was the originator and developer of the science of Ichnology, and this collection is the largest and most valuable of its kind in the world. It now consists of 21,773 tracks of animals of 120 different species, all belonging to the general name of Lithichnozoa, or Stone-track animals.[58] Most of the slabs were taken from stone-quarries at Turner's Falls, South Hadley, and Holyoke. Complete reports of the discoveries were prepared by President Hitchcock, and submitted, in 1853 and 1865, to the State. Among the most interesting of these slabs, as one passes through the room, is the large horizontal stone at the left, marked with the tracks of the great "Oto-zoum." It was found at Mount Tom station; and on the table beside it is the reverse of the impression. This enormous animal had the bulk of an elephant and the build of a toad. On the wall, behind the bust of President Hitchcock, is a set of specimens which prove the animals making these tracks to have been quadrupeds. The marks show the fore-feet, the trace of the tail and the hind-feet, with imprints of the heels, as if the animal had crouched down on the soft mud. On the stairway wall is another interesting stone, which has the footprints of an animal that had lost one of its toes, the impressions showing first a two-toed, and then a three-toed foot. In the first wall case are the only bones of the track-making animals ever found in Massachusetts. The next slab at the left, standing on edge, shows impressions of the feet of an enormous animal, the tracks being a foot long, and between them running a great tail-trace. The large, framed slab has interest because it was used a long time as a flagstone. Near it hangs the egg and leg-bones of an existing bird of New Zealand. They were placed there at the time the track-making animals were thought to be birds: at the present time they are generally believed to have been reptiles.

The next slab is marked by the feet of an enormous three-toed bird; the imprints will hold a gallon of water, and are three times the size of those of an elephant. The central one of the side rooms contains, on the walls and tables, a collection of slabs remarkable for the great variety of insect tracks. More insect tracks and the most perfect footprint of a reptile, ever found, are in the last side room. The footprint shows plainly all the wrinkles of the epidermis of a three-toed foot. Under the windows in this room are stones marked by rain-drops, one of them showing the steps of a lizard-like reptile, who turned a sharp corner in his haste, throwing his tail outside of the row of his footprints. There are several specimens of what President Hitchcock designated as "stone books" here. They show the same footprint through a number of layers of stone, and when split open form a book, the leaves of which fit into one another.

The Gilbert Museum of Indian relics is placed in the first of the three small rooms. There are four hundred specimens of the stone implements used by the North American Indians, especially those of the Connecticut Valley. The collection took the name of the Hon. George H. Gilbert of Ware, who contributed largely toward the expense of gathering it.

Passing out of the main entrance of the Cabinet, the brick building at the right is

The South College Dormitory. This is the oldest building on the college grounds, originally containing both recitation and living rooms. Its corner-stone was laid in the summer of 1820 by the trustees of Amherst Academy, and the building completed in a little more than three months, the dedication occurring in September of the year following. The institution was then known as the Amherst Charitable Institution. Noah Webster, president of the Academy, and afterward president of the trustees of the Institution, delivered the oration at the laying of the corner-stone. The building is 100 feet long and 30 wide, and cost $10,000, raised by subscription. Much of the material used in the construction was contributed by persons living in Amherst and the neighboring towns, even at the distance of twenty-five miles. On one occasion these acceptable gifts were received just as work was about to be suspended for want of material to carry it on. At present the building contains thirty-two double rooms. In the summer of 1891 extensive alterations were made in this building, steam heat and other improvements being introduced, and the suites of rooms so arranged that each student might have a well-lighted bedroom; provisions made to accommodate three or four students who desire to occupy a common room as a study. The views from the windows of some of the upper rooms are magnificent.

The Chapel and dormitories.

The College Chapel, next to the South College Dormitory, was built in 1827, and bore for some time the name of Adam Johnson of Pelham, who bequeathed money for its erection. The suits at law conducted by the college authorities to establish the validity of the will reduced the legacy to $4,000, and $11,000 had to be raised from other sources. The building measures 100 by 56 feet. For many years it accommodated all the departments of instruction in the College. Dr. Tyler says that beside the Chapel proper, the "building originally contained four recitation rooms, a room for philosophical apparatus, and a cabinet for minerals on the ground-floor, two recitation rooms on the second floor, a library on the third floor, and a laboratory in the basement." The basement was the chemical workshop of Professor Hitchcock, afterward president of the College. The arrangements have been very little altered since then. The two rooms on the second floor form now the small chapel, and the rooms above are seldom used. In the main chapel, morning prayers are held. The seniors are assigned the seats in the centre of the room hall, the juniors on their right, and the sophomores on their left. The gallery is for the freshmen and visitors.

In favorable weather the ascent of the College Chapel tower will repay the visitor. There are ninety-eight steps to climb, and the summit commands a magnificent view of the Connecticut Valley. The stone step in the main doorway of the building is 358 feet above sea-level. The clock in the tower was presented by L.H. McCormick, '81. The next building,

The North College Dormitory, was built in 1822, after the same plan as South College. Until the erection of the Chapel, daily prayers were held in rooms in the building. Its cost was $10,000. Whenever the demand for rooms warrants, this building will be altered in the same manner as was South College. On the knoll, in front of the North College Dormitory, is situated

Woods Cabinet and Observatory.

The Woods Cabinet, with the College Observatory and the geological lecture rooms adjoining. The building stands upon the site of the first meeting-house of the First Congregational Society. The Cabinet and the Observatory were built in 1847 at a cost of $9,000, which was raised by subscription, the name of Hon. J.B. Woods of Enfield being given to the Cabinet, and that of Hon. Abbott Lawrence to the Observatory, in recognition of their bequests to the College. The geological lecture room was added in 1855, and cost $1,000; and two years afterward Enos Dickinson of South Amherst gave the Dickinson Nineveh Gallery, which for twenty-seven years held the sculptured slabs now in the hallway of the College Library. The collections in this building cover the whole subject of geology and mineralogy. The main room on the lower floor contains a collection valued at $10,000, illustrating the geology of the Western Hemisphere, with particularly complete collections from Massachusetts and Connecticut. The large collection of minerals in trays is not open to public inspection. On the second floor is the Shepard collection of meteorolites, and in the gallery a very large collection illustrating the geology of the Eastern Hemisphere.

The Observatory consists of an octagonal tower, 50 feet high and 17 feet in diameter, with a revolving dome and a central pedestal supporting a telescope with an aperture of 7½ inches and a focal lens of 8½ inches. The telescope was presented by Hon. Rufus Bullock of Boston, and cost $1,800. In the transit room, 13 by 15, is a transit circle built by Gambey of Paris, the telescope having a focal length of about 3 feet and an aperture of 2½ inches.[59]

The new, more powerful Observatory, 1905. *Image courtesy of editor's collection.*

PRATT FIELD, on Northampton and Orchard streets, about a quarter of a mile from the college buildings, comprises about thirteen acres of land presented for athletic purposes in 1890 by Fred B. Pratt, of Brooklyn, a graduate of the class of 1887. The field is laid out with a quarter-mile oval track, a hundred-yards straight-away track, and a short track for jumping. A handsome grand-stand, designed by William B. Tubby of New York, and having a seating capacity of six hundred, was erected in 1891 at the west end of the oval. It contains ample conveniences for the use of the college teams, including dressing-rooms and baths. Other portions of the field are to be laid out for lawn tennis and other out-of-door sports. The entire field cost about $20,000, of which about $9,000 was the price of the grandstand, all being the gift of Mr. Pratt.

Hallock Park, on the opposite side of the railroad cut, belongs to the College: most of it was a gift of Leavitt H. Hallock, of the class of 1863.

On the further side of Snell Street is Blake Field, which for many years was the only athletic field of the College. To Lucien I. Blake, of the class of 1877, belongs the credit of acquiring this field. In 1876 he gathered about $900 from the alumni of the College, paying the $600 additional in a mortgage in the name of the athletic association. In 1890 this debt was assumed by the trustees. The first athletic field of the College is now included in Pratt Field. It was sold to the Massachusetts Railroad, who at first proposed to lay their track through it, and recently re-purchased.

The Grandstand on Pratt Field.

## The Fraternity Houses

Nine of the many Greek-letter fraternities of the country are represented among Amherst College students. In order of their establishment here, they are: Alpha Delta Phi, Psi Upsilon, Delta Kappa Epsilon, Delta Upsilon, Chi Psi, Chi Phi, Beta Theta Pi, Theta Delta Chi, and Phi Delta Theta. This number is probably larger in proportion to the size of the College, than can be found at any similar institution in the United States; but notwithstanding this, the college authorities are unanimous in believing that Amherst has been benefited, intellectually and socially, by the presence of these fraternities. Thus far, any well-recognized fraternity has found its efforts to establish a chapter at Amherst warmly seconded by the faculty, although, on account of the rapid increase during the last few years, it is hardly probable that this policy will be continued. During the few years directly following the establishment of the earlier chapters, the sentiment of the College generally opposed the idea of secrecy, and the open literary and debating clubs were very formidable rivals for society honors. At the present time the open societies have disappeared, with one exception, and more than eighty-two per cent of all the members of the College belong to the Greek-letter fraternities. The actual numbers of students in college and members of the fraternities, since 1889, when the last chapter was established here, are shown by the accompanying table:

1888–89, 358 students in college, 299 members of fraternities
1889–90, 344 students in college, 281 members of fraternities
1890–91, 352 students in college, 289 members of fraternities

The following letter of Ex-President Julius H. Seelye, printed in the *Century Magazine* for September, 1889, gives an admirable idea of the advantages of the societies to their members, as well as of their position and relations to the College:

> *Others can give a more accurate opinion than I upon college fraternities elsewhere; but so far as Amherst is concerned there can be only a favorable judgment concerning them by any one well informed. Without a doubt they exercise here a wholesome energy, both upon their individual members and upon the College. Combination is strength, whether with young men or old; and where men combine for good ends, better results may, of course, be looked for than where the same ends are sought by individuals alone.*
>
> *Now the aim of these societies is certainly good. They are not formed for pleasure simply, though they are one of the most fruitful sources of pleasure in a student's college life. Their first aim is the improvement of their members,—improvement in literary culture and manly character. They are all of them literary societies. An effort was made not long since to introduce among us a new society, with prominently social, rather than literary aims; but it not only failed to receive the requisite assent of the president of the College, but was not favored by any considerable number of the students, many of whom stoutly opposed it.*
>
> *One of the happiest features of society life at Amherst is connected with the society houses. There are no better residences in the village than these, and none are better kept. They are not extravagant, but they are neat and tasteful; they have pleasant grounds surrounding them; the cost of rooms in them is not greater than the average cost in other houses, and they not only furnish the students occupying them a pleasant home, but the care of the home and its surroundings is itself a culture.*
>
> *There need be no objection to these societies on account of their secrecy. The secrecy is largely in name; it is, in fact, little more than the privacy proper to the most familiar intercourse of families and friends. Treated as the societies are among us, and occupying the ground they do, no mischief comes from their secrecy. Instead of promoting cliques and cabals, in point of fact we find less of these than the history of the College shows before the societies came. The rivalry between them is a healthy one, and is conducted openly and in a manly way.*
>
> *The societies must give back to the College the tone they have first received. I am persuaded that in any college where the prevailing life is true and earnest, the societies fed by its fountain will send back bright and quickening streams. They certainly give gladness and refreshment to our whole college life at Amherst.*

All of the fraternities represented at Amherst have chapter houses, and in most cases own them. These buildings are large enough to accommodate at least a portion of the members beside providing parlors, reading-rooms, and a lodge room for general use. The chapters of Chi Psi, Psi Upsilon, and Alpha Delta Phi now own the entire southern end of the square bounded by the village Common, Northampton Street, and South Prospect.

The members of the fraternities are usually glad to welcome their friends for the inspection of the houses at any time, excepting only on Tuesday evenings, which are universally observed as "society nights."

Presuming that visitors to Amherst have acquaintances in each fraternity ready to become their hosts, the following order will be found convenient for a tour of the houses:

The Delta Kappa Epsilon (Sigma Chapter) house is situated on Oak Grove Hill, Lessey Street, a short walk east from the Amherst House. The original portion of the house and the grounds were purchased by the chapter in 1885, and the new part added the same year. Together they now accommodate eighteen students. The Delta Kappa Epsilon fraternity was founded in 1844 at Yale University, and in 1890 had thirty-one chapters and about eight thousand members. The Amherst Chapter was organized in 1846, the original members being six students of the class of 1848. The quarters of the chapter have been successively in North College, Cook's Block, and the present dwelling-house of W.H.H. Morgan on Maple Avenue. The chapter has thirty-four active and more than five hundred alumni members, among the more prominent of these latter being General F.A. Walker, president of the Massachusetts Institute of Technology; Judge I.H. Maynard, assistant secretary of the Treasury in President Cleveland's administration; Charles Hallock, editor of Forest and Stream; Melvil Dewey, librarian of the State of New York,[60] Rufus G. Kellogg, donor of the Kellogg prizes in Amherst College.

Delta Kappa Epsilon House.

Returning to the Amherst House, and proceeding in the direction of the College, at the right are the

Alpha Delta Phi (Amherst Chapter) houses, which occupy the lot on the corner of Pleasant and Sellen streets, and extending back to North Prospect Street. The new house was erected in 1890, and is a three-story and basement building, the materials used being Elyria sandstone, pressed brick, and terra cotta. On the first floor are drawing, banquet, and reading rooms; while the two upper floors furnish accommodations for eighteen members of the chapter. The house stands some distance back from the street, and faces the village Common. The chapter also owns the lot of land in the rear of this house, fronting on South Prospect Street. The old house stands in the rear of the new one, facing the side street. Originally a dwelling-house, it was purchased by the society in 1874. It was the first chapter house to be established in Amherst, and contains rooms for sixteen students. The Alpha Delta Phi fraternity was established in 1832, by Samuel Eels, and has a membership of over five thousand. The Amherst Chapter was the first chapter of a Greek-letter fraternity to be established at Amherst, and its total membership is a little over five hundred. The active membership of the chapter averages about thirty-three.

Among the alumni of the chapter the names of Rev. Henry Ward Beecher, Rev. Roswell Dwight Hitchcock, Rt. Rev. Frederic Dan Huntington, Rev. Richard

Salter Storrs, Rev. Edward Hitchcock (president of Amherst College from 1845 to 1854), Hon. John E. Sanford, and Rev. E. Winchester Donald are prominent. Next to the Alpha Delta Phi houses, and facing the village Common, is the

Alpha Delta Phi House.

Psi Upsilon (Gamma Chapter) house. The building was erected as a residence for the first president of the College, Rev. Zephaniah S. Moore, and was the "President's House" until 1833. Its corner-stone was laid by Noah Webster, and the trustees of "The Collegiate Charitable Institution," September 18, 1821, directly following the inauguration of President Moore and the dedication of South College. It was bought by the chapter in August, 1879, and now accommodates fourteen students. The Gamma Chapter was established in 1841, by sixteen members of the classes of 1842, 1843, and 1844. For some years it was virtually a junior class society. The first rooms were in South College; and later, after one or two changes, in Cutler's Block. This latter building was burned July 3, 1879, destroying nearly all the possessions of the chapter. In 1890 the chapter bought the adjoining estate on the corner of the Common and Northampton Street, intending to erect here a second building. The Psi Upsilon fraternity was founded at Union College in 1833, and in 1891 had 17 chapters and about 7,000 members. In that year the Gamma Chapter had 38 active members and 425 living alumni, among whom are Ex-President Julius H. Seelye of Amherst College, Dr. Charles H. Parkhurst of New York, Ex-Governor Andrews of Connecticut, Hon. George B. Loring of Washington, Arthur S. Hardy of Hanover, N.H., Professor Herbert B. Adams of Johns Hopkins University, President H.H. Goodell of the Massachusetts Agricultural College, and Henry D. Hyde,

Psi Upsilon House.

Esq., of Boston. On the corner of Northampton and South Prospect streets, adjoining the grounds of the Psi Upsilon Chapter, is the

Chi Psi (Alpha Chi) Lodge, erected in 1884, after plans made by Robert S. Stephenson of New York. The Alpha was founded in November, 1864, by members of the classes of 1864, 1865, and 1866, and owns, in addition to the lot on which the house is situated, the estate in the rear, known as the Burt place. The membership is small, rarely exceeding six men from each class. The Chi Psi fraternity was founded at Union College in 1841, and has Alphas in sixteen colleges, embracing in their membership about three thousand men. The lodge contains rooms for thirteen members, beside ample parlors, library, and room for fraternity purposes. The fraternity is represented in public life by Chief Justice Fuller, Ex-Speaker T.B. Reed, J. Sterling Morton, and Ex-Postmaster General Dickinson, and among other members are Commodore Elbridge T. Gerry, Hugh Cole, Esq., Francis M. Scott, Frederick D. Tappan, William Astor of New York, General Duane, late Chief of Engineers, U.S.A., President Thomas W. Palmer of the Columbian Exposition, President Brainard of Middlebury College, and Robert Earl of the New York Court of Appeals.

On the right, further down Northampton Street, stands the

Theta Delta Chi (Mu Deuteron Charge) house, which was purchased by the charge in 1889, and an addition made in the summer of 1890. The charge was founded in 1885, by twenty-four members of the classes of 1885, 1886, 1887, and 1888, and for five years occupied the second and third stories of Dickinson's, and the adjoining block, Pleasant Street. The present house accommodates twenty students, and the membership of the charge in 1891 was thirty-five undergraduates and fifty-one alumni.

The Theta Delta Chi fraternity was founded at Union College in 1846, and comprised, in 1891, nineteen charges. Before the war the fraternity was very strong in the Southern States, but it is now represented in that section almost solely by its alumni.

Returning to the corner of Northampton Street, and crossing the Common, the building on the left corner of College Street is the

Theta Delta Chi House.

Beta Theta Pi (Beta Iota Chapter) house, purchased for a chapter house in 1886, and accommodating twenty of the members. The chapter grew out of a local society, the "Torch and Crown," which was founded in 1878 by members of the class of 1881, and in the fall of 1879 occupied the present Theta Delta Chi chapter house, on Northampton Street. The "Torch and Crown" received a charter from the Beta Theta Pi fraternity in 1883, and was made a chapter of that fraternity. In 1891 the fraternity had sixty chapters, and over nine hundred and fifty undergraduate members.

Among its prominent members are Secretary of the Interior, John W. Noble; Justices James M. Harlan, Stanley Matthews, and William B. Woods, of the Supreme Court of the United States; besides ten United States senators, forty United States representatives, fifteen State governors, and six ministers to foreign countries.

Proceeding down College Street, the second house at the left is the

CHI PHI (Phi Chapter) house, built in 1885 by the chapter, then of nine years' standing. The building is of the Queen Anne style, and furnishes apartments for eleven students. From the time of the organization of the chapter until the present house was completed, the headquarters were in Palmer's Block, which once occupied the site of the town hall. The Chi Phi fraternity was founded in 1854, at Princeton College, and now has twenty-two chapters. Among the one hundred and sixty alumni and active members of the Phi Chapter are Hon. Henry Stockbridge, '77, of Baltimore, Md., and the Rev. H.H. Kelsey, '76, of Boston, who had much to do with the institution of the chapter.

Beta Theta Pi House.

Chi Pi House.

Further down this street, and opposite the home of Ex-President Seelye, is the Phi Delta Theta (Massachusetts Beta) house. The chapter was founded May 9, 1888, with twenty-three members from the classes then in college, and at once leased its present building and grounds of their owner, Professor W.C. Esty, securing the right of future ownership. It was the sixty-fifth chapter of the fraternity, which was founded at Miami in 1848. During the War of the Rebellion the chapter-roll was reduced to five; and two of these were the causes of the reawakening of the fraternity. The organization is controlled by a general council and province presidents, whose power is absolute within their spheres,—a convention of the chapters once in two years, and a province convention once in two years. In 1891 there were sixty-six undergraduate and twenty-four alumni chapters, the whole membership being 6,803 undergraduates and alumni. The fraternity numbers among its members Benjamin Harrison, President of the United States.

The only remaining fraternity house is situated on South Pleasant Street, and to reach it the visitor should return to the corner of Northampton Street, and pass College Hall, the Library, and dwelling-houses, on the way to the Central Massachusetts station.

The Delta Upsilon (Amherst Chapter) house was purchased in 1882, thirty-five years after the founding of the chapter. The rooms first occupied were in South, and later in North, College. The chapter was re-established in 1869, a hall being fitted up in Palmer's Block, which stood on the site of the town hall. Four years after, the chapter moved to quarters in Kellogg's Block, where a hall and several suites of rooms were occupied by the members, until the present house was entered. The Delta Upsilon fraternity was founded in 1834 at Williams College, and the Amherst Chapter in 1891 numbered twenty-nine active and 334 alumni members. Among the latter are: Rev. George Washburn, president of Robert College, Constantinople; Rev. Daniel Bliss, president of the Protestant College at Beirout, Syria; William Swinton, author of Swinton's educational works; Rev. Hiram C. Hayden, president of Adelbert College, Cleveland, O.

Chapter 6

# The Agricultural College

The Massachusetts Agricultural College was one of the first institutions of its kind to be founded in the United States. By an act passed July, 1862, Congress granted to each State a portion of the public lands, the money from the sale of which, it was provided, should go toward establishing and maintaining at least one college where "the leading object shall be, without excluding other scientific studies, and including military tactics, to teach such branches of learning as are related to agriculture and the mechanic arts, in order to promote the liberal and practical education of the industrial classes in the several pursuits and professions of life." The State legislature formally accepted this grant April 18, 1863, and afterward set aside one-third of it for the Massachusetts Institute of Technology at Boston. The trustees for the Massachusetts Agricultural College were incorporated by an act of April 29, 1863, and they found their share of the Congressional grant to be 360,000 acres of land, which afterward yielded $146,000.[61] The corporation organized with Governor Andrew as president, A.W. Dodge, Esq., vice-president, and Charles L. Flint, secretary; but in 1864 the legislature changed the legal name of the institution to the Massachusetts Agricultural College, and Hon. Henry E. French of Cambridge was elected president, the Governor remaining an ex-officio member of the board of trustees. The question of the location of the College provoked much discussion among the parties interested. The decision came when the town of Amherst promised $50,000, and sufficient land at a reasonable rate, the trustees accepting the offer May 25, 1864, and the Governor and Council approving the choice soon after. The present estate of the College—383½ acres[62]—was then purchased at a cost, including the buildings then standing, of about $43,000. The erection of the first college buildings was authorized by the trustees May 26, 1866.[63] In this year President French resigned, and was succeeded by the Hon. Paul A. Chadbourne, who in his turn retired the following year because of ill health. The work of the trustees up to this time had been simply preparatory to the opening of the College, and, therefore, the list of actual presidents may be said to commence with President Clark, who succeeded President Chadbourne. The terms of office of the presidents were as follows:

Colonel William S. Clark, Ph.D., LL.D, 1867–1877
Charles Louis Flint, A.M., LL.B, 1879–1880
Hon. Levi Stockbridge, 1880–1882

Hon. Paul Ansel Chadbourne, (Second Term) 1882–1883
James Carruthers Greenough, M.A., 1883–1886

President Henry Hill Goodell was the acting president during six months of 1883, and in July, 1886, was elected to the position which he still holds.

The College was opened for students October 2, 1867 the entering class numbering thirty-three. The instructors numbered four. Before the close of the term there were fourteen more students.

The faculty comprised, in 1891, twelve members exclusive of the president. This body has the general direction of the College in matters relating to the curriculum and to discipline.

The State Board of Agriculture constitutes a board of overseers of the College, and through their special committees make frequent examinations of the work and condition of the institution. Their annual reports are submitted to the legislature, and are published as public documents.

The degree of Bachelor of Science is awarded to successful graduates, the governor of the Commonwealth signing the diploma. By a special arrangement between the authorities of the College and the Boston University, the former has become the Agricultural Department of the University, and receives its students in that science. Students of the Agricultural are permitted to matriculate with the University, and on graduation may receive its degree of Bachelor of Science, in addition to that of the College, thus obtaining the privileges of alumni in both institutions. A military diploma is granted at the discretion of the professor of military science and tactics.

The course of study at the College is entirely prescribed, and is largely scientific in its nature. There are ample provisions, however, for the study of literature and the languages.

Generous financial aids are offered to students who wish to obtain an education at a small expense. As nearly all the scholarship funds of the College have been established by the legislature, students coming from homes within Massachusetts are favored before those from other States. In addition to the following specified sums, $5,000 is devoted each year to the payment of those who perform work in the various departments. About $120 is given annually in prizes. The scholarships are: eighty State scholarships, established by the legislature of 1886, $10,000; fourteen Congressional, established by the trustees, $1,120; private bequests (the income of $3,000) amounting to $150. Application for one of the State scholarships is made to the State senator of the district in which the student resides; and for a Congressional scholarship, to the representative to Congress.

The necessary expenditures of a student in college are estimated as closely as possible in the accompanying table. It is assumed in these that the student actually pays for each item, any beneficiary money which may be credited to him by the College, or any other means which may be adopted to reduce the cost of an education, not being taken into consideration. It is believed that the estimate in the "Least" column may be followed without injurious deprivation of any kind. The students are required to room in the college dormitories, and with a room-mate; the items of rent, furniture, fuel, and light are reduced by being shared. The actual cost

| | LEAST. | MODERATE. | AMPLE. |
|---|---|---|---|
| Tuition . . . . . . . . . | $80.00 | $80.00 | $80.00 |
| Books and Stationery . . . . | 8.00 | 12.00 | 20.00 |
| Room Rent . . . . . . . . | 24.00 | 36.00 | 48.00 |
| Furniture (annual average) . . | 8.00 | 15.00 | 25.00 |
| Board . . . . . . . . . . | 90.00 | 108.00 | 126.00 |
| Fuel and Light . . . . . . . | 11.00 | 15.00 | 25.00 |
| Washing . . . . . . . . . | 10.00 | 15.00 | 25.00 |
| Clothing . . . . . . . . . | 30.00 | 60.00 | 100.00 |
| *Military Suit . . . . . . | (15.75) | (15.75) | (15.75) |
| Society and Class Taxes . . . | 3.00 | 8.00 | 15.00 |
| Subscriptions . . . . . . . | — | 5.00 | 10.00 |
| Sundries . . . . . . . . . . | 15.00 | 25.00 | 40.00 |
| Boston University Course . . | — | 10.00 | 10.00 |
| *Laboratory Fee . . . . . | (30.00) | (30.00) | (30.00) |
| Totals . . . . . . . . . | $279.00 | $389.00 | $524.00 |

* Each of these items occur only once during the college course, and are not included in the totals.

of these items to each student is therefore entered in the estimates. In the rent of the higher-priced rooms, steam heat is included.

The military department of the College is under the direction of an officer of the United States army, detailed to the position by the Secretary of War. Instruction in military drill tactics is made one of the requirements of the College by the act of Congress providing for the establishment of the institution. Each student, not physically incapacitated, is thus under the surveillance of the commandant. The cadet battalion, organized with four companies, is officered by the students of the upper classes; and the drills are held three times each week. Recitations upon the tactics and the art of war, and practical instruction in target, artillery, and mortar practice are features of the department. During the sessions of the College, the rooms of all the students are inspected once a week by the commandant. Most of the arms and ammunition used in the battalion are provided by the United States. The military diploma, awarded by the commandant at the satisfactory completion of the college course, recommends the receiver to an office if volunteer troops are ever called for by the State authorities.

Connected with the Agricultural College in their aims, yet distinct in organization and work, are the State Agricultural Experiment Station and the Hatch Experiment Station. These are so nicely arranged that they supplement each other in their experiments, neither one attempting the same line of investigations as the other, although in several instances the same person is in charge of similar departments in the College and in both of the stations. This plan lessens the necessary expenses, and increases the funds available in every department of experiment, resulting in unusually large returns in proportion to the outlay. The organizations of the two departments are here given.

The Massachusetts STATE AGRICULTURAL EXPERIMENT STATION was established in 1882, by an act of the legislature, passed May 12 of that year. The Station was located at the State Agricultural College, forty-eight acres of land being leased from the College, and its management was vested in a board of control of seven members, the governor of the Commonwealth being president *ex officio.* The sum of $3,000 was first appropriated for equipping the new station, and $5,000 a year thereafter granted for its maintenance. This annual grant was increased in 1885 to $10,000. The objects of the investigations of the Station were fully set forth in the original act as follows: "The causes, prevention, and remedies of the diseases of domestic animals, plants, and trees. The history and habits of insects destructive to vegetation, and the means of abating them. The manufacture and composition of both foreign and domestic fertilizers, their several values, and their adaptability to different crops and soils. The values, under all conditions, as food, for all farm animals, for various purposes, of the several forage, grain, and root crops. The comparative value of green and dry forage, and the cost of producing and reserving it in the best condition. The adulteration of any articles of food intended for use of men or animals; and in any other subjects which may be deemed advantageous to the agriculture and horticulture of the Commonwealth."

After the organization of the Board of Control of the Experiment Station, Charles A. Goessmann, Ph.D., LL.D., was elected director and chemist, which positions he has held ever since. The director has six trained assistants in the chemical work and one in the field. The membership of the Board of Control was increased in 1888 to eleven. They are elected for terms of years,—two from the members of the State Board of Agriculture, two from the Board of Trustees of the State Agricultural College, one from the Massachusetts Society for promoting Agriculture, one from the Massachusetts State Grange, and one from the Massachusetts Horticultural Society, appointed by the respective organizations, and the president of the State Agricultural College, the director of the Station, and the secretary of the State Board of Agriculture. This Board of Control submits to the legislature, through the director of the Station, an annual report of its investigations, twenty-five thousand copies of which have been printed each year since 1889. The Station also issues occasional bulletins of ten thousand copies each, and monthly statements of official analyses of commercial fertilizers during the months of April and October of every year.

The work at the Experiment Station is limited only by the amount of money available. Each new source of revenue opens a corresponding channel of investigation. The annual income amounts to $16,500, of which $10,000 is received from the State, $5,000 from the Hatch Experiment Station in return for doing the entire chemical work of that institution, and about $1,500 from certificates issued to dealers in commercial fertilizers as required by law.

The grounds of the State Experiment Station are leased from the Agricultural College, at merely nominal rental, for a period of ninety-nine years, and comprise forty-eight and one-half acres, of which ten are woodland. Seventeen and three-quarters acres are on the west side of the county highway, and thirty and a half on the east side. The buildings of the Station are valued as follows:

Chemical Laboratory (with fixtures), $15,000
Agricultural and Physical Laboratory (two), $12,000
Farmhouse, $2,000
Barn and Feeding Stables (with fixtures), $6,000

The Hatch Experiment Station of the Massachusetts Agricultural College was organized in 1887 under the provisions of the Hatch act, which passed Congress and was approved by the President, March 2, of that year. The act established experiment stations in all the States and Territories of the Union, with the object of promoting "scientific investigation and experiment, and the principle and application of agricultural science." For each station the annual appropriation of $15,000 was granted; of the first year's income, not more than twenty per cent, and the years following, not more than five per cent, of this sum might be used for erecting buildings for the Station. The president of the Agricultural College, Henry H. Goodell, A.M., was elected director, and Frank E. Paige, of Amherst, treasurer of the Station, which positions they have held ever since. The departments of the Station, as now established, are Agriculture, Horticulture, Entomology, and Meteorology. The Station is always engaged in investigations important to the farmer and other classes in the State. Quarterly bulletins of about eleven thousand copies are issued. Of the annual income, $5,000 is paid by the Station to the chemical department of the State Experiment Station, where all the work of that kind is performed. The property of the Hatch Experiment Station is divided among the various departments as follows:

Agricultural (barn), $4,000
Horticultural (greenhouses), $2,800
Entomological (insectary), $2,000
Meteorological (apparatus), $1,800

## The College Buildings

The Agricultural College is situated on North Pleasant Street, about a mile from the village of Amherst. Lying upon the western slope of Mount Pleasant, it overlooks the entire Connecticut Valley, within the boundaries of the prehistoric lake. The extensive grounds are always admirably kept, and the buildings offer many things of interest to the visitor. The distance is convenient for a pleasant walk or drive, and as the institution has been considered by the leading agriculturists who have visited it from the United States and Europe, as the finest in this country, it certainly should not be neglected.

In making the tour of the college buildings, it will be found most convenient to enter the grounds by the way of Amity Street and Lincoln Avenue, or by North Pleasant Street, in either case commencing with the college barn, at the left, and following the course marked out in this book.

The first building to be noticed is the

College Barn, built in 1869, and altered to its present form in 1889; valued at $14,500. The building contains the specimens used for illustration in the department of agriculture in the College. For this purpose there are typical specimens of farm stock, representing the different breeds of horned cattle and swine, a valuable stallion, and a small flock of sheep. The apparatus for farm work is very complete.

The building is so neatly kept as to be attractive even to persons who have no special connection with agricultural affairs. In the management of the college farm it is intended to illustrate the systems and methods best suited to the conditions of this locality, and in all the operations the possible educational effect is kept prominently in view. While labor on the farm is not compulsory, not a little is performed by the students, and every opportunity is given to any who specially desire instruction in any particular line of farm work to obtain it. The dwelling-house adjoining the barn is occupied by the superintendent of the college farm and his assistants.

Some distance southward from these buildings, and just beyond the boundaries of the college grounds, is the D.G.K. Society house. This was bought in 1891, from Professor C.D. Warner, whose residence it was.

The next building is the

Drill Hall, erected in 1883, at an expenditure of $6,500, a legislative appropriation for the purpose. The Armory, at the right of the entrance, contains the arms furnished by the State to the college corps of cadets. The main hall is 123 feet long and 48 feet wide, and has an asphalt floor. It is heated by a hot-water system, introduced in 1888. This comfortable winter quarters of the corps is used by the students as a gymnasium. The second floor of the building contains the commandant's office, and a recitation room for the classes in military-tactics science. A short stairway leads into the tower of the building. On the campus adjoining this building are earthworks for use in mortar practice—a part of the regular military training of the College.

The Drill Hall.

On the right is the

College Chapel, completed in 1886, at a cost of $31,000, which was provided for the purpose by special legislative appropriations.[64] The material used in construction is Pelham granite, with brownstone trimmings. The two entrances at the south end of the building lead into the alumni headquarters, and by winding staircases to the hall above. The college library occupies the main portion of the lower floor. This contained, in 1891, about ten hundred volumes, and its rate of increase during the past three years has been twelve hundred volumes annually. The president's office is situated on this floor. The second story forms a hall capable of seating six hundred people, and here the Sunday services of the College, and the commencement exercises are held. The building is heated by steam and lighted by electricity.

Agricultural College Chapel and Library.

South College Dormitory.

The South College Dormitory, beyond, was first built in 1867, and contained several recitation rooms and the college library. On February 4, 1885, it was destroyed by fire, and rebuilt in 1886, at a cost of $37,000, a special appropriation by the legislature. The building is brick, three stories in height, and contains twenty suites of double rooms for students. The south wing overlooks the college campus and parade ground. In the north wing are recitation rooms and the museum of the biological department. The collection in this museum contains representatives of every type of American animal, and is valued at about $3,500. The office of the Hatch Experiment Station is in the tower of this building.

The meteorological observatory of the Hatch Experiment Station is also located in the tower. The observatory was established by money granted under the Hatch Experiment Stations act of Congress, and it is modelled as nearly as possible after the Central Park observatory in New York City. Observations were commenced by Professor C.D. Warner, the first and present director, on January 1, 1889. The instruments in use are all of the Draper self-recording pattern, which ordinarily require the attention of the observer not oftener than once a week. The most important of them is the electrograph, which was constructed after Professor Warner's design by Elliott Brothers, London, England. It measures the electric potential of the atmosphere, and keeps a record by a delicate and continuous photographic process. The instrument, when received by the observatory in October, 1890, was considered the most delicate and the most complicated ever constructed.

The instruments in the observatory, and their cost, are as follows:

Electrograph, $600
Mercurial barometer, $250
Evaporimeter, $240
Sun thermometer, $175
Direction of wind, $175
Force of wind, $175
Rain-gauge, $175
Thermometer, $30

North College Dormitory.

The meteorological department issues monthly and annual bulletins of its observations, and these are sent to any one who applies for them. In 1890 the monthly circulation of the bulletins numbered 400. Next is noticed the

North College Dormitory, completed in the fall of 1868. Its cost was $36,000, and sixty-four students may be accommodated in it. The college reading-room is on the first floor.

Just behind this building is the

Laboratory Building, the first of the college buildings, erected in 1867. Originally a two-story building, it has been altered, now being valued at $10,360. It now contains the chapel, used for morning prayers, the laboratory of the zoological department, and a part of the chemical department, on the first floor; the rooms of the mathematical, physical, and chemical departments, on the second; and an interesting collection of agricultural implements from Japan in the third. This last story was formerly the drill hall of the cadet battalion, and is now used as a museum until a special building is erected.

Across the ravine is the residence of the college pastor, and next to it is a

Boarding-House, built by the College in 1868, costing $8,000. For a number of years it was managed by the college authorities, but in 1891 was in the hands of a boarding-club of sixty students. The house accommodates the family in charge of the practical details.

The Barn, of the Hatch Experiment Station, is in the rear of the boarding-house. Built in 1889, and costing $4,000, it is used for experiments in feeding farm stock, and in other matters of importance to the farmer. The building was burned in the spring of 1891 and immediately rebuilt.

Following the road as it completes the circle of the college grounds, the visitor finds himself before the

Chemical Laboratory of the State Experiment Station, built of brick and sandstone. It faces to the south. The main building is two stories in height, measures 30 by 42 feet, and has a tower projecting from the southeast corner. Two parallel wings, each one story high and 32 feet long by 19 feet wide, join the rear of the building. The main house contains, on the ground-floor, the director's office, assistants' room, two small weighing-rooms, and passages leading into the wings, which are used as laboratories. Of the rooms on the upper floor, one is occupied by the assistants, and the other three are used for storing collections illustrating various agricultural industries. The building was erected in 1883, after plans suggested by the director, and made by E.A. Ellsworth, a graduate of

The Chemical Laboratory.

the College. Its cost was $15,000, including the apparatus it contains. Of this sum, $11,500 was a legislative appropriation, the rest coming from the regular income of the Station. The entire chemical work of both the Massachusetts State and the Hatch Experiment stations is carried on in this laboratory.

The Farmhouse and barn of the State Experiment Station are situated about one hundred and fifty yards north of the chemical laboratory, and are valued together at $8,000. The house and main barn were built before the farm passed into the hands of the State, and has been re-modelled from time to time since. Here resides the farmer of the Station, who is in general charge of the farm work under the superintendence of the director. The barn contains the seed-room, grainroom, silos, scales for weighing the crops, and live stock. In 1886 the feeding-stable and first wing were added, and shortly after another stable and wing of the same size were built in the rear of the first. Experiments in feeding and digestion that have been carried on here are among the most important to farmers of all that the Station has undertaken. A visit to the barn cannot fail to be of interest. Everything is kept in most perfect order and neatness. The buildings are subject to frequent change, depending upon the nature of the questions under investigation. The creamery attached to the barn was built in 1887, and the ice-house of one hundred tons' capacity was erected at the same time.

Just across the town highway from the Chemical Laboratory stands the

Agricultural and Physical Laboratory of the State Experiment Station, a brick building, two and a half stories high, with brownstone trimmings, and a frontage of forty feet, and a depth of thirty-five feet. This was the first building in this country erected for the special purpose of studying the more intricate questions of plant growth with reference to agricultural plants, and the relation of fungus growth to plant diseases. It was completed early in 1890, at a cost of $10,000, appropriated by the State legislature. Its outfit cost nearly $3,000. The second floors are divided into four, of equal size each. The lower floor is devoted to microscopic investigations. It contains an office with two laboratories and a photographic studio, supplied with an overhead railroad for bringing large plants from the shed to the camera. The second story is occupied by the assistant superintendent of the field and feeding experiments. He has an office, and a chemical laboratory for studying the physiological condition of the soil, and a private apartment. In the rear of the building, and connecting with it, is a covered shed, twenty-five feet square; a glass house, of the same size; and a greenhouse, twelve feet wide, and forty feet long. From the open side of the covered shed, three parallel railways extend sixty feet on to the grounds. Within the shed are turn-tables and tracks, which lead into the glass house; and altogether they furnish a very convenient method of transporting the plants under investigation to and from the open air. This system of connecting shed and glass houses and photographic studio by means of railways is modelled upon a plan used by Dr. Hellriesgel, at Beruburg, Germany. The building was designed, in conformity with special instructions, by E.A. Ellsworth of Holyoke, a graduate of the College. It is maintained by a portion of the funds of the Hatch Experiment Station.

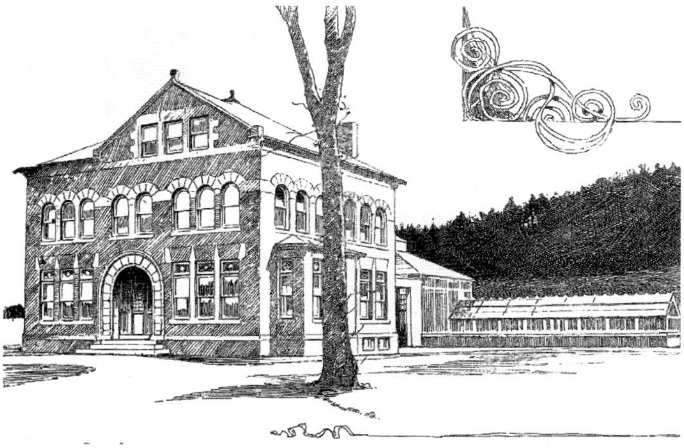

The Agricultural and Physical Laboratory.

Following the college road as it turns again in the direction of the town, the dwelling-house at the right is the home of the professor of horticulture. Beyond is the

Botanic Museum of the College, built in 1866, at a cost of $5,180. It is a two-story frame structure, 43 by 45 feet, and was one of the four buildings erected about the time of the opening of the College. On the first floor is a laboratory and recitation room. On the floor above is the Knowlton Herbarium, collected by W.W. Denslow of New York, of fifteen thousand species, one of the finest collections in the country. A large collection of native woods, and fifty specimens of wood from the Himalaya Mountains, made by the celebrated travellers, the Von Schlagentwelt brothers, are also kept in this room.[65] One of the most interesting objects in the room is a cast of a mammoth squash, grown in the plant house in 1873, which actually lifted, in the course of its growing, a weight equal to forty-five hundred pounds, and for some days after an accidental cracking of the shell supported five thousand pounds. The office of the college treasurer is in this building, his hours being from four to five o'clock one or two afternoons of each week.

The neighboring stable was built in 1885 for the use of the horticultural department of the College, cost $1,500, and is conveniently arranged for the use of the department.

The President's House, on the hill-side, was built in 1884 for the use of President Greenough, and cost $11,500. It is still the property of the College, and occupied as a residence by W.P. Brooks, professor of agriculture.

On the land between this building and the stable, the horticultural department makes experiments in growing small fruits and berries. A fine vineyard is at the north of the president's house, and a large peach orchard and a nursery at the east. These contain many of the finest varieties of vines and trees, which are cultivated entirely for experiment.

The Durfee Plant House, a gift of the late Dr. Nathan Durfee of Fall River, at one time treasurer of the College, was built in 1868 at an expense of $12,000. On January 23, 1883, the house was partially destroyed by fire, but was immediately rebuilt, and is now valued the same as originally. The main house consists of an octagon, 40 feet in diameter, and two wings each 60 feet long and 30 wide. A workroom in the rear of the octagon communicates with two parallel pits each 50 feet long. A small wing, 24 by 16 feet, opens from the northeast corner of the octagon. The main house contains many types of plants for illustration and educational purposes. These are provided from the income of a $10,000 fund, the gift of the late Leonard M. Hills and his son Henry F. Hills, of Amherst. The pits and the small wing are used for growing marketable plants and flowers.

The Greenhouse of the Hatch Experiment Station was constructed in the fall of 1888, after special plans devised by Professor S.T. Maynard, the head of the horticultural division. Completely fitted, it cost $2,800, and is designed for experiments in plant-growing, with different methods of heating. There is a main room, containing the heating apparatus, and two parallel greenhouses of exactly the same size and construction, extending from the south side. One of them is heated by steam, and the other by hot water. Valuable investigations are made here each winter, and the results widely published.

The grounds at the south of this group of buildings is used by the horticultural department for experiments in fruit and ornamental tree-culture. The farmhouse on the opposite side of the road is one of the buildings bought with the land at the time of the establishment of the College. The small building at the left is the

Insectary of the entomological department of the Hatch Experiment Station, built in 1889. The expense of its construction, $2,000, was met by the Agricultural College and the Massachusetts Society for the Promotion of Agriculture. The investigations of this department relate to the life and habits of insects injurious to vegetation, and are under the direction of the State entomologist, Professor Charles H. Fernald. The building is a story and a half high, 28 by 20 feet in area, and has

The Insectary.

adjoining it a greenhouse 30 feet long and 18 wide. The ground-floor contains the entomologist's office, a laboratory, and an "insecticide room," where the various compounds for killing insects are tested. The laboratory occupies the entire half of the floor adjoining the greenhouse. This latter is divided into a hot room and a cold room, which are used for breeding insects. In the cellar of the main house are vaults for wintering such insects as may be under investigation. It was in this building that the extended investigations of the gypsy moth, for the destruction of which the State has expended much money, were first made. The department is constantly receiving queries from all over the country, principally this State, however, in regard to the destruction of common and injurious insects.

# Noteworthy Business Firms

*Editor's note*: Advertisements at the end of books were fairly common in the nineteenth century. Often they were for other books available from the same publisher. Worth noting in this section is the fact that six of the advertisements are for Boston firms. Also interesting is the advertisement for this very book, which was self-published by Hitchcock.

**DEAN, WHEELOCK & CO.,**

*Wholesale and Retail Dealers in*

**ARTISTIC PAPER HANGINGS and CEILING DECORATIONS.**

LEADS, OILS, VARNISHES, AND PAINTERS' SUPPLIES.

ALL KINDS EXTERIOR AND INTERIOR PAINTING AND DECORATING DONE TO ORDER.

267 Main Street, Opposite Academy of Music, Northampton, Mass.

---

JAMES DOOLING,

Caterer and Confectioner

11 and 13 TEMPLE PLACE, BOSTON, MASS.

---

MRS. L. E. REDDING,

**Students' Boarding House.**

*Board, $4.00 per week. A few Good Rooms to rent.*

CORRESPONDENCE PROMPTLY ANSWERED.

MAPLE AVENUE, - - - - AMHERST.

---

JOHN MULLEN,

DEALER IN

PROVISIONS, FISH AND OYSTERS,

CANNED GOODS, ETC.

UNION BLOCK, - - - AMHERST, MASS.

---

MILAN W. BULL,

DEALER IN

Breech-Loading Shot Guns, Rifles, Revolvers,

**Fishing Tackle, Ammunition. * Lawn Tennis and Base Ball Goods a Specialty.**

Repairing promptly done on Guns, Pistols, Umbrellas, Parasols, etc., etc. All styles of Stencil Cutting, and General Jobbing.

No. 445 MAIN STREET, Opposite Court Square.

# Notes

## Author's Introduction

1. William A. Dickinson was Emily Dickinson's older brother. Her father, Edward Dickinson (1803–1874), was treasurer of Amherst College from 1835 to 1873, and was a United States congressman from 1853 to 1855. He was also active in Massachusetts state politics.

## Chapter 1

2. The author meant Thomas Hooker (1586–1647), the English Puritan preacher who arrived in Boston in 1633. It was the minister Cotton Mather who called him the "light of Western churches."
3. Not "the" mid-eighteenth-century French and Indian War of most history books; the author is referring to an earlier conflict.
4. One rod is equal to 16.5 feet. Rods were commonly used as a unit of measurement in colonial times.
5. In 1798 alone, eleven Amherst boys were attending college (eight of them at Williams).
6. Jeffrey Amherst (1717–1797) was a British hero of the French and Indian War. The name Amherst is from the Saxon *Hemhurste*, meaning "wood's edge." The Amherst family had been prominent in England since at least the early thirteenth century. Jeffrey Amherst was serving as an officer in Germany when he was made a major general and called to aid the British against the French in North America. He found fame with a victory at Louisbourg (on the island of Cape Breton in the North Atlantic) in 1758. The colonial governor of Massachusetts at the time, Thomas Pownall, was a close friend of Amherst's, so he named the new district after him. Jeffrey Amherst went on to capture Montreal in 1760, and was knighted in Staten Island in 1761. He was also made commander in chief of all British forces in North America for a time, before he returned to his estate in his

native England. Jeffrey Amherst is said to have played a part in spreading disease among Native Americans by approving the dispensing of germ-laden blankets to the native population. The Lord Jeffrey Hotel on the Common in Amherst was opened in 1926.

7. Ebenezer Kellogg kept an inn from 1734 to 1737 and again from 1752 to 1757. His brother Ephraim kept inn from 1744 to 1756. In 1738, it was voted to give Ebenezer Kellogg three pounds and seventeen shillings to provide rum and sugar for the raising of the Amherst meetinghouse.

8. The reference is to Oliver Wendell Holmes (1809–1894).

9. The Dickinson family arrived in the New World in the seventeenth century and grew rapidly in both importance and size. There was at least one Dickinson among the members of the Hadley Selectmen in 1660, 1664, 1665, 1666, 1668, 1669, 1673, 1675, 1676, 1678, 1680, 1683, 1685, 1687, 1689 and 1690. Once Amherst was settled, the Dickinsons became prominent there as well. One 1783 Amherst petition (relating to the formation of a new parish) was signed by twenty Dickinsons.

10. William S. Tyler's *History of Amherst College During its First Half Century* was published in 1873.

11. Noah Webster (1758–1843) was famous for compiling a popular dictionary. He lived in Amherst from 1812 to 1822, while he worked on his dictionary. In 1822, he left Amherst with his family. His home was then turned into a hotel, which burned down in February 1838. He is buried in New Haven, Connecticut.

12. According to Tyler, the road was so muddy at times it was impassable. At this time, the Amherst Common was part swamp and part pasture; on the east side was a goose pond.

## Chapter 2

13. Mabel Loomis Todd (1856–1932) was a writer and neighbor of Emily Dickinson. She helped bring Dickinson's poetry to publication after her death, and edited several collections of Dickinson's poetry.

14. The Victorian sensibility for aesthetics was not so much a factor during colonial times. Settlers built their homes and outbuildings according to their needs at the time, and panoramic considerations were likely not included.

15. The mansard roof, a French Second Empire style that was adopted by the Victorians from the 1860s to the 1880s, was apparently looked upon with disdain at the time (at least by the author). Now, however, remaining homes with mansard roofs are viewed as architectural treasures.

16. This poem has four more lines that were not included:

> "The lower metres of the year,
> When nature's laugh is done,—
> The Revelations of the book
> Whose Genesis is June."

17. Four lines of his poem were omitted after the line ending "haze":

A few incisive Mornings,
A few Ascetic Eves,—
Gone, Mr. Bryant's "Golden Rod,"
And Mr. Thomson's "sheaves."

Four more lines were omitted at the end of the poem:

Perhaps a squirrel may remain,
My sentiments to share.
Grant me, Oh Lord, a sunny mind,
Thy windy will to bear!

18. This was the first time these two Emily Dickinson poems had been published in book form. Interestingly, it is in the section written by Mabel Loomis Todd, Dickinson's posthumous editor and champion, that the poems excerpts appear. Though Dickinson had achieved some measure of posthumous fame by the 1890s, her legend had not yet grown to what it is today. In an 1896 book on Amherst, Emily Dickinson was the seventh writer listed in a section on Amherst authors, following two Amherst College presidents and a professor.

19. Edward Tuckerman (1817–1886), born in Boston, was a professor of botany at Amherst College from 1855 until his death.

20. William Cullen Bryant (1794–1878) was a journalist and poet. Besides his Massachusetts house, he also had an estate known as Cedarmere at Roslyn on Long Island.

21. Henry Ward Beecher (1813–1887) was an 1834 graduate of Amherst College.

22. Charles Dudley Warner (1829–1900), a writer, was born in Plainfield, Massachusetts, and wrote *My Summer in a Garden*.

23. Jenny Lind (1820–1887) was first brought to prominence in the United States by P.T. Barnum.

24. George Washington Cable (1844–1925) was a novelist, the author of *Madame Delphine*, among other works.

25. H.H. was how the writer Helen Hunt Jackson (1830–1885) was commonly known. Born Helen Maria Fiske in Amherst, she was the daughter of a professor at Amherst College. She became a well-known poet and author of several fiction and nonfiction books, including the novels *Mercy Philbrick's Choice* (1876) and the popular *Ramona* (1884), as well as an exposé of government treatment of Native Americans called *A Century of Dishonor* (1881).

26. William Pynchon (~1590–1662) arrived at what is now Springfield in 1636.

27. Mount Holyoke College was founded in 1837.

28. Smith College was founded in 1871.

29. On September 18, 1675, soldiers from Hadley were ambushed by Indians. Dozens of soldiers were killed. Reinforcements managed to send the attackers away, but the "Bloody Brook" massacre left Deerfield badly shaken and the settlement was briefly abandoned.

30. Before coming to the New World, General William Goffe and General Edward Whalley had signed the death warrant of King Charles I in 1649. They were wanted men once the deceased king's son took power in England.
31. Deerfield was attacked on February 29, 1704. Numerous homes were burned and 41 settlers were killed, while 111 were taken captive.
32. Daniel Shays (1747–1825) was captured, tried, convicted, sentenced to death and then pardoned. He later moved to New York state.

## Chapter 3

33. No mention is made here of the bridge between Northampton and Hadley, because the "drive" does not call for a river crossing at Northampton. However, the bridge was an important connection between Amherst and Northampton throughout the nineteenth century. The original bridge was built in 1807 at a cost of $14,294. It was rebuilt in 1817 and 1826, and had repairs in 1840 and 1848. In 1859, a flood destroyed the bridge and it was rebuilt for $20,000. The bridge was partially destroyed by a hurricane in 1879 and once again was rebuilt.
34. Northampton was originally known as Nonotuck. It was first settled in 1654 and incorporated as a city in 1884.
35. A dam broke due to heavy rain, causing major flooding.
36. Interestingly, Sunderland barely rates a mention in Hitchcock's book. Prior to its incorporation in 1718, Sunderland was known as Swampfield. It hardly seems possible there was nothing of particular interest in the Sunderland of 1891 to merit a mention. Tobacco was an important crop in nineteenth-century Sunderland. Sunderland's River Road today contains many fine old homes. It also is the location of the Sugarloaf Estates apartment complex that provides housing for many UMass students. Sunderland also offers the only Connecticut River crossing between Hadley and Greenfield.
37. A hotel was built atop the mountain in 1864 by Dwight Jewett.
38. The company bought out the Chubb Fishing Reel Company of Vermont in 1891 and continued to expand. In 1927, it changed its name to the Montague Rod and Reel Company.
39. He published a *Catalog of Choice Selected Flower Seeds and Bulbs.*
40. Josiah Gilbert Holland (1819–1881).
41. One of the biggest changes to occur in the Amherst area since *The Handbook of Amherst* was published was the creation of the Quabbin Reservoir during the 1930s. The eighteen-mile-long reservoir holds 412 billion gallons of water. Four towns were abandoned and flooded to create the reservoir: Enfield, Dana, Greenwich and Prescott; a dam was built at the Belchertown end of the reservoir.

## Chapter 4

42. The Massachusetts Central Railroad was incorporated in 1870 to build and operate a railroad through Northampton, Easthampton, Westhampton, Hatfield, Hadley, Amherst, Granby, Ludlow, Belchertown, Ware, Palmer and points farther east.
43. One politician born in Amherst was Silas Wright Jr. (1795–1847), who was a state senator, United States representative, Unites States senator, Massachusetts state comptroller and governor of New York. Another was Gideon Lee (1778–1841), who went on to become mayor of New York City from 1833 to 1834.
44. There were fifty-one members of the Amherst Club when it was founded. Other clubs of the 1890s included Ramona, a women's club founded in 1893; the Eagle Lodge of the New England Order of Protection, founded 1890; Pacific Lodge F. and A.M., founded 1801; the Rod and Gun Club, founded 1888; and the Nonotuck Cycle Club, founded 1895.
45. The first printing press was brought to Amherst in 1825. The first newspaper, the *New-England Inquirer* (subscriptions cost two dollars per year), was printed December 1, 1826. One story on the cover page reported on a cattle show in New Hampshire.
46. Emily Dickinson attended Amherst Academy and graduated from there in 1847.
47. The Goodell House, built 1875, was later the residence of the poet and Amherst College professor Robert Frost, who lived there for about fifteen years.
48. Incorporated 1850. In 1855, there were eight hundred life members of the society.

## Chapter 5

49. Not mentioned here is the Antivenenean Society (Society Against Poison) that was formed at Amherst College during the summer of 1830. Members pledged that they were "convinced that it is best for us to dispense with Ardent Spirit, Wine, Opium and Tobacco as articles of luxury or diet…we hereby pledge to one another our mutual promise that while connected with this Institution we will abstain entirely from these articles except as Medicines, and the use of Wine at the Lord's Supper." Out of the 208 students at the College, 118 signed the pledge in 1830. Through 1863, about 75 percent of Amherst College students joined the temperance society.
50. Among those families with multiple Amherst graduates during the first forty years of the college's existence were Adams, Allen, Bliss, Chapin, Clapp, Clark, Dickinson, Eastman, Howland, Humphrey, Kimball, Lyman, Perkins, Pratt, Richardson, Smith, Taylor, Tyler, White and Williams. By 1921, 33 Dickinsons had attended Amherst College. Famous nineteenth-century Amherst College graduates include President Calvin Coolidge (1895); Chief Justice Harlan F. Stone (1894);

William R. Mead, founder of the famous architectural firm of McKim, Mead & White; and the future abolitionist Henry Ward Beecher (1834). Many Amherst graduates went on to distinguished careers. By 1921, there were more than 1,000 (not including those who attended but did not graduate) who had become ministers; 1,600 who had become authors, editors or journalists; about 500 college professors; over 500 doctors and surgeons; nearly 1,000 lawyers; 100 judges; more than 250 state senators or legislators; over 100 publishers and newspaper owners; 23 members of Congress; and 8 governors.

51. As of 1857, there were a cumulative total of 1,237 alumni of Amherst College, 1,036 of whom were still living, and 512 professors, of whom 446 were still living. By 1863, there were a total of 1,520 graduates of Amherst College, of whom 1,261 were living, and 610 professors, of whom 516 were living. A total of 2,807 students attended Amherst College up to 1863, but 1,326 (47 percent) did not graduate, either for lack of money, lack of scholarship, homesickness or transfer to another college.

52. Yearly tuition was about $30 in 1821 and $110 in 1891.

53. College Hall was remodeled in 1905 by the architectural firm of McKim, Mead & White.

54. The President's House was remodeled again in 1932 by the firm of McKim, Mead & White.

55. The Amherst College art collection (more than sixteen thousand pieces) is now housed in the Mead Art Museum, built 1949.

56. Walker Hall was demolished in 1963 to make way for the new Frost Library, built in honor of Robert Frost, who was a professor at Amherst College on and off between 1917 and his death in 1963. President Kennedy spoke at the groundbreaking in October, just a month before his assassination.

57. Natural history specimens were accumulated for Amherst College at a breakneck pace during the nineteenth century. For example, in 1853–54, 224 fossils from Germany and Silesia, 50 species of fossil fish and several casts of dinosaur bones were obtained for $200.

58. Dr. Hitchcock was perhaps the first to prove the existence of dinosaurs, yet all along he believed the fossil footprints he had located to be those of ancient birds. He did not believe in evolution, and rejected Darwin's theories, instead trying to explain fossils and the earth's geology without discarding creationism. In 1852, he wrote a book called *The Religion of Geology and its Connected Sciences*. He began that work with the statement, "The leading object, which I propose in the course of lectures which I now commence, is to develop the relations between geology and religion." Still, in his lifetime, he collected more than twenty thousand fossil footprints and greatly enriched the collections of Amherst College and, at the same time, the knowledge of the scientific world.

59. A new and more powerful observatory was constructed in 1905 (see illustration).

60. Melvil Dewey (1851–1931) created the Dewey Decimal Classification system of cataloguing library books.

## Chapter 6

61. Massachusetts Agricultural College became known as Massachusetts State College in 1931, and then as the University of Massachusetts in 1947.
62. The University of Massachusetts Amherst campus now comprises 1,450 acres and has an enrollment of 23,500 students.
63. The entering class of students in 1867 numbered forty-seven. There were six professors in the early years. One of the earliest experiments of the students at the new college had to do with the cultivation of sugar beets. The first graduating class, in July 1871, numbered twenty-seven. The governor attended the ceremonies.
64. The Old Chapel, as it is known today, still stands. The University of Massachusetts book collection now has its own home in the massive, twenty-six-story-tall W.E.B. Du Bois Library, designed by Edward Durrell Stone.
65. The correct spelling is von Schlagintweit. The three brothers, Hermann, Adolf and Robert, had studied the Alps, among other areas.

# Bibliography of Additional Nineteenth-century Resources


Carpenter, Edward W., and Charles F. Morehouse. *The History of the Town of Amherst, Massachusetts, 1731–1896*. Amherst, MA: Press of Carpenter & Morehouse, 1896.

Hitchcock, Edward. *Reminiscences of Amherst College, Historical, Scientific, Biographical and Autobiographical*. Northampton, MA: Bridgman & Childs, 1863.

Holland, Josiah Gilbert. *History of Western Massachusetts: The Counties of Hampden, Hampshire, Franklin, and Berkshire*. Springfield, MA: Samuel Bowles and Company, 1855.

Judd, Sylvester. *History of Hadley, Including the early History of Hatfield, South Hadley, Amherst & Granby, Massachusetts*. Springfield, MA: H.R. Hunting & Company, 1905.

Montague, W.L., ed. *Biographical Record of the Alumni of Amherst College, During its First Half Century, 1821–1871*. Amherst: 1883.

# About the Author

Born in Boston in 1867, Frederick Hitchcock's career as a writer and publisher was just beginning when he wrote *Handbook of Amherst* in 1891. In fact, he had just graduated from Amherst College when the book was published. Hitchcock would eventually move to New York City and publish numerous and varied genealogies and town histories. In 1901, he founded the Grafton Press. The process of publishing and marketing books interested him; while at Grafton, he edited a book titled *The Building of a Book: A Series of Practical Articles Written by Experts in the Various Departments of Book Making and Distributing* (1906). Other typical books he published were *Ancestors of Charles Dana Bigelow and his Wife Eunice Ann Howe*, by Josephine Frost (1926), and *Songs and Ballads of the Anthracite Miner: A Seam of Folklore Which Once Ran Through Life in the Hard Coal Fields of Pennsylvania* by George Korson (1927). He died in 1928.

# About the Editor

Richard Panchyk received a master's degree in anthropology from the University of Massachusetts at Amherst in 1994, while living in nearby Sunderland. He also pursued doctoral studies at the University of Massachusetts. He is the author or coauthor of twelve books, including *Engineering the City* (2001), *World War II for Kids* (2002), *Galileo for Kids* (2005), *Our Supreme Court* (2006; foreword by Senator John Kerry), *Franklin Delano Roosevelt for Kids* (2007; foreword by Senator Edward Kennedy) and *A History of Westbury, Long Island* (2007). He has also written numerous encyclopedia and journal articles. His works have been translated into Portuguese, Chinese, Korean and Japanese.